The Wandering Mind

The Wandering Mind

Understanding Dissociation from Daydreams to Disorders

John A. Biever, MD
and
Maryann Karinch

ROWMAN & LITTLEFIELD PUBLISHERS, INC.
Lanham • Boulder • New York • Toronto • Plymouth, UK

Published by Rowman & Littlefield Publishers, Inc.
A wholly owned subsidiary of The Rowman & Littlefield Publishing Group, Inc.
4501 Forbes Boulevard, Suite 200, Lanham, Maryland 20706
www.rowman.com

10 Thornbury Road, Plymouth PL6 7PP, United Kingdom

British Library Cataloguing in Publication Information Available

Library of Congress Cataloging-in-Publication Data

Biever, John A., 1947–
  The wandering mind : understanding disassociation, from daydreams to disorders /
John A. Biever and Maryann Karinch.
    p. cm.
  Includes bibliographical references.
  ISBN 978-1-4422-1615-0 (cloth : alk. paper) — ISBN 978-1-4422-1617-4 (ebook)
  1. Consciousness. 2. Dissociation (Psychology) 3. Mental health. I. Karinch,
Maryann. II. Title.
  QP411.B54 2012
  612.8'233—dc23   2012013303

♾™ The paper used in this publication meets the minimum requirements of
American National Standard for Information Sciences—Permanence of Paper
for Printed Library Materials, ANSI/NISO Z39.48-1992.

Printed in the United States of America

We dedicate this book to Dr. Saroj K. Parida

Contents

Foreword

Dr. Mark Whitacre, "The Informant"

$\mathscr{A}$t the core of our mental lives lies a paradox. Our senses have evolved to provide us with a detailed perception of the outside world; at the same time, our brains often don't process this information as it is received. We log mental records—absolutely certain of their accuracy—that combine genuine sensing with distorted perception, imagination, or extrapolation. With no intent to concoct a lie and no desire to mutate facts, our minds simply wander from reality.

Often that wandering happens at the worst times. When we should be concentrating on a task, conscious of details and sensitized to next steps, we find that our focus has been hijacked. We are misdirected to a daydream or a trance-like state; while often enjoyable, it removes us from the reality of our present circumstances. Pleasurable fantasy at best, dangerous and destructive distraction at the worst. Wouldn't we expect natural selection to have eliminated this as a feature of the human mind? Failure of individuals to see the world as it really is can lead to unintended disastrous consequences and even personal failure.

In this book, Dr. John Biever and Maryann Karinch provide an extraordinary glimpse into the world of dissociation, from normal experiences to the extreme condition called dissociative identity disorder (DID), in which multiple personalities emerge. The authors marshal evidence, spanning everything from neuroscience to group dynamics to relationships of adults with children, of an arms race between the conscious and unconscious mind. At times, nearly all of us daydream, and the authors lead us from understanding the value and harm of such normal dissociations all the way to grasping nuances of the phenomenon called DID.

My good friend, Dr. Saroj Parida, a well-known neonatologist, is afflicted with DID and brings to the text extremely valuable insights into this disorder. Saroj has lived with DID for more than forty years in a fleeting world of altered reality. Having taken full responsibility for insurance fraud committed while under the influence of alters, he is now serving an eight-year sentence in a federal prison. He is determined to help others by relating his own experiences. As a child, Saroj was sexually abused by a caregiver over a ten-year timeframe and in order to cope with the abuse, his mind learned to escape into multiple identities. In effect, his mind enabled him to adapt to the horror by creating another reality for himself. As an adult, Saroj functions as a fully competent physician; nonetheless, he lapses into alters as his subconscious dictates.

"Escape" is the animal instinct for survival that has remained intact despite millions of years of human evolution. It is the flight part of a "fight-or-flight" response to trauma that any of us could face at any time. Physical escape is not possible for a child. So, he or she must escape mentally. Every child is born with some innate capacity to escape (nature), but the environment (nurture) also plays a significant role. Escape can be viewed comically as the embarrassment experienced by the characters in the "Got to Get Away" Southwest Airlines TV commercials. It can also be viewed tragically as in post-traumatic stress disorder (PTSD) suffered by war veterans, fire fighters, law enforcement officers, and yes, victims of childhood sexual abuse.

Intelligent, accomplished people like Saroj face two kinds of bias when they "escape" into pathologic states and get a diagnosis of mental illness. First of all, depending on the type of condition, some people will dismiss the diagnosis as a fancy way of saying "eccentric" or "self-absorbed." Secondly, many will jump to the assumption that, if the person is so smart, then how could he or she let a thing like that take hold? Surely, they recognize symptoms. Surely, the illness could not be "responsible" for their committing a crime because, well, they're too smart for that!

These biases are in full bloom when it comes to dissociative disorders. Is it really possible that people might not remember days or even years of their life, or wander off to a different town and not know how they got there, or have other personalities that sometimes emerge without their knowing it consciously?

When journalists pander to the popular taste for sordid stories about "crazy people," they exacerbate the misunderstanding about mental illnesses. Case in point: the controversy over the story of Shirley Ardell Mason, a.k.a. Sybil. A 2011 book[1] purports to expose the Sybil story as a scam, a case of misdiagnosis of multiple personality disorder that ultimately evolved into a sensationalistic book and movie of the same title. The popular media response to this book zoomed right past the reality that some people actually do have multiple personalities. Skeptics about the diagnosis felt vindicated, and acceptance and understanding of a serious mental illness took a giant step back to the sixteenth century.

In this book, John and Maryann give us cases, descriptions of symptoms, scholarship, and an in-depth look at both diagnostic and treatment procedures for extreme dissociative conditions. Even armed with those, we still can't "see" dissociation. It doesn't show up as a spot on a scan or the image of a misshapen region inside the brain. Whether good or bad, normal or abnormal, it's invisible. So I ask you to plunge into the evidence, open your eyes as you travel to a deeper state of understanding—and believe.

Dr. Mark Whitacre is an Ivy League PhD and the highest-ranked executive of any Fortune 500 company in U.S. history to become a whistleblower. He was responsible for uncovering the ADM price-fixing scandal in the early 1990s. Suffering from an undiagnosed bipolar disorder, he embezzled funds from ADM during the time he was aiding FBI investigations of the company. The movie The Informant!, *starring Matt Damon as Dr. Whitacre, is based on that time of his life.*

Acknowledgments

JOHN BIEVER

𝓘n opening a book for the first time, I used to go to the table of contents, or to the first page of text, or to the foreword or introduction. The "Acknowledgments" were a nice private gesture of the author to those who contributed in varied ways to the writing. But I've changed. And I believe that the essence of my joy at reading the acknowledgments has evolved from my gratitude to all of those whose contributions of time, wisdom, and/or practical advice—for no personal material gain—enable and enrich the final product. So I'm very grateful to you—may I acknowledge you!—for giving me the opportunity in this reading to share with you my indebtedness to the following people.

My special thanks goes to my wonderful coauthor, Maryann Karinch, whose curious—and sometimes delightfully wandering—mind has enriched the substance and form of this book in innumerable ways. May we have the opportunity to collaborate again!

Thank you to the true experts in the field of dissociation and dissociative disorders, particularly to the late Herbert Spiegel, MD, and his son David Spiegel, for their seminal work in clinical hypnosis, and to Richard Kluft, MD, for his extraordinarily lucid writing and teaching about the devastating effects of childhood trauma and the developmental evolution and treatment of dissociative identity disorder.

And while I'm thanking the experts, I extend a very special thanks to my good friend and colleague Daniel A. Hughes, PhD, whose elegant treatment methodology for children with horrific early life experiences is embodied in his writings and teachings. His compassion for all of us sharing the human condition is truly infectious, and I can only hope that I've spread the infection to you in the manner of my writing.

Any psychiatrist who decides to stick his neck out by making public his views on a controversial issue had better be prepared for those inclined to take a whack at it. My inspiration in this regard came from my departmental chair in psychiatry residency, Dr. Anthony Kales, whose courage in publicly advocating his beliefs about good patient care, often against the tide of prevailing opinion within the profession, continues to serve me as a model for forthright commitment to advocating the best of clinical care. Thank you, Dr. Kales. You're hereby an honorary leatherneck!

I want to thank my patients and their parents whose graciousness in allowing me to share their stories is truly noble—you know who you are, so please feel beyond the veil of confidentiality the gratitude of those who read these words!

I have the luxury in my clinical practice at Quittie Glen of meeting regularly for mutual supervision with a group of skilled and seasoned colleagues, whose ongoing reflection on the cases I've described in this book has both inspired me to persevere in the difficult treatments and provided sage practical suggestions. So my thanks go to Elizabeth Montagnese, MD; Matthew A. Biever, DO; Charles P. Gilbert II, ACSW; Dale K. Horst, MA; and Douglas A. Ockrymiek, DO.

I have received great inspiration from a man I've never met, but whose acquaintance I feel I've made nevertheless through my treatment of Dr. Parida. This man is Mark Whitacre, whose international fame and importance have not prevented him from graciously and continuously providing warm personal support for my patient. Mark, I am forever and deeply indebted to you for the many ways in which your friendship of Saroj has facilitated my work with him.

And, finally, I thank in the most special way, of all my patients, whose identity will not remain anonymous—Saroj K. Parida, MD, whose story winds its way through the book and will continue to unfold, I'm certain, in a most fascinating way in the years that lie ahead. He has taught me, Maryann, and everyone with ears that can truly listen and eyes that can truly see, that a responsible and steadfast approach to one's mental illness can become a uniquely beautiful gift to self and others.

MARYANN KARINCH

*T*hank you, John, for the pleasure of producing this book with you; writing with you and learning from you seemed much more like fun than work. Of course, we could never have done this without Saroj Parida, a most extraordinary man, talented physician and artist, and a great friend—the one who initiated the whole project! Sincere thanks also to a wonderful and emotionally generous man, Mark Whitacre; you and Ginger have shown amazing grace.

I deeply appreciate the encouragement, intelligent questions, and support I received from Jim McCormick, my mother, brother, and friends, all of whom expressed tremendous interest in the subject matter, which I talked about incessantly. Acknowledgments also to Greg Hartley, my friend and valued coauthor (of seven books), whose insights on human behavior are often dazzling; Anju, Kurren, Rishi, and Anisha—Saroj's beautiful family; Becky and Doug Losee, who were so giving of their time; and my pals, Holly and Cindy, who are always cooking with good ideas. I also want to thank Dr. Robert Oxnam, the renowned China scholar whose honest and riveting discussion of his own dissociative identity disorder in *A Fractured Mind* added another dimension to my understanding of the adaptive phenomenon of dissociation.

Sincere thanks also to Suzanne Staszak-Silva, Melissa McNitt, and everyone at Rowman & Littlefield who has supported this book with great enthusiasm and intelligence.

Introduction

Doubt is an uneasy and dissatisfied state from which we struggle
to free ourselves and pass into the state of belief; while the latter
is a calm and satisfactory state which we do not wish to avoid,
or to change to a belief in anything else.

—Charles Sanders Peirce, founder of pragmatism
"The Fixation of Belief," *Popular Science Monthly,* 12
(November 1877)

I believe that every book is a story. If the book *isn't* a story, at the least it
has a story. And I believe that all stories are ultimately moral tales. Yes, even
textbooks. Even scientific treatises. Even research papers. So I hope you will
look for and find the story in this book and the moral tale within it. Finally,
I believe that all good stories manage somehow to be enjoyable to read. And
despite the seriousness and importance of the topic, I believe that the enjoying reader will get the most out of it. Oscar Wilde had it exactly right: "Life
is too important to be taken seriously."

The Wandering Mind is a story about the human experience of dissociation, a state of mind almost as mysterious and unsettling as it is com-
monplace. It seems our human brain is uniquely wired in a way that propels
our mind to attempt to understand our inner and outer worlds, and to gain
that understanding by way of a collection of *beliefs.* Beliefs are so wonderful
because they enable us to satisfy the constant demand of our brain for understanding, and in the deal, the brain spares the mind of painful emotions
like confusion, anxiety, worry, and despair. (Clearly I believe that the brain
and the mind are separate, albeit related, parts of us; the former, physical and
the latter, essentially social. I like to think of the brain as "the home base of
the mind" from which the mind ventures out into the world of experiences

1

with others . . . or fails to. Modern scientific investigation of brain function is revealing which parts of the brain are on the "frontier" of reaching out to other brains through mental life.)

Belief is also so wonderful because it enables us to get along despite *doubt*, which is another annoyance wired into the human brain whose redeeming purpose seems to be to protect our mind from the hazards of false certainty ("I *believe* Susan when she tells me that her dog Killer will not bite me when I try to pet him, but— "). Without belief, we would never get into a car, take a bite of food, or reach out to a friend for help. Because there's no certainty that any of those actions will not result in a bad outcome. Indeed, when doubt is too strong and belief too weak, we can become paralyzed from taking necessary actions in our lives. This is one way of understanding the common psychiatric problem called *agoraphobia*, wherein afflicted persons remain "safely" at home all the time in order to avoid the "unacceptable" risk of venturing out into the world.

But sometimes it is doubt that is too weak and belief too strong. And the consequences can be just as mischievous as the reverse. Let's say Roy is driving to the shore to begin his long-awaited vacation. His mind goes into a delightful daydream: he's lying on the beach, shoving a cold beer into the foam sleeve he got at the Phillies game. Now he sees Utley's walk-off home run all over again. Now he's back on the beach, trying to keep the seagulls away from his fries, hearing that foamy fuzz bubbling up from the sand as the waves recede, thinking that's the same sound the club soda will make this evening as it lands on his scotch and ice cubes, feeling the sun giving him that mild burn he'll have to fight off at dinner beneath his brand new Tommy Bahama® shirt. Then suddenly, the daydream ends, and Roy finds himself twenty miles beyond the expressway exit. Meanwhile, Sally missed half of the lecture on the use of differential equations to analyze climatic effects on the nineteenth-century middle-European textile industry because she was daydreaming about her upcoming trip to the shore where—you guessed it—she was going to meet up with Roy! Daydreams are one of the most common examples of *dissociation*, which in essence is a temporary state of disconnection from conscious awareness of the usual sensory (vision, hearing, bodily sensation, etc.) or internal (thought, feeling, memory, etc.) input. Roy was not temporarily blind, nor Sally deaf. Nevertheless their minds were consciously unaware of what their brains took in from their sense organs.

What does this all have to do with *doubt*? As we will see, dissociative experiences vary on a full spectrum from relatively harmless everyday experiences such as Roy's and Sally's to potentially devastating kinds and degrees of dissociation, referred to in the *Diagnostic and Statistical Manual of*

Mental Disorders as "dissociative disorders." But almost without exception, the more serious the dissociative disorder, the more unusual—sometimes verging on unbelievable—the dissociative symptoms become. A woman experiences a type of dissociation referred to as a "fugue state" and winds up in a remote town with no memory for who she is. A man's personality disintegrates—dissociates—into several personalities, each totally or partially unaware of the others.

Most of us have heard the old quip, "Of all the things I've lost, I miss my mind the most." We are indeed terrified of losing our minds, so terrified that we may cling to the belief that these serious kinds of dissociation do not really exist; that is, that they are simply imagined by persons with weak or immature minds, or even faked. In other words, in order to adhere to a comfortable *belief*—that dissociative disorders do not exist and therefore we will never suffer one—we do not hold up that belief to sufficient *doubt*. And in so doing we sacrifice on the altar of false certainty the open-minded curiosity about the nature of the mind and dissociation that is so necessary in order to yield true understanding.

Further, to the extent that we need to cling to a belief, we may be prepared to sacrifice others who believe otherwise on that same altar. Sadly, the psychiatric profession itself bore witness to this calamity in the early days of the diagnosis of multiple personality disorder. During a period when the psychiatric community felt the influence very heavily of German leaders in the field, a doctor named Edmund Stengel attacked the prevailing notion that multiple personality disorder was a real condition. So for a while after the 1943 publication of his argument—based in opinion, not science—the disorder "disappeared" and those in the profession who felt compelled to diagnose and treat it felt discredited. Eleven years later, after what was essentially a blackout on journal coverage of the illness, psychiatrists Corbett H. Thigpen and Hervey M. Cleckley wrote about Christine Costner Sizemore. Known as the case providing the story for *The Three Faces of Eve*, Sizemore's true story stands as a landmark in raising public awareness of—and belief in—the existence of multiple personalities. As of this writing, Sizemore is still alive and her diagnosis remains unquestioned.

My inspiration to write this book evolved from my experience in treating the most unusual patient I'd encountered in my now twenty-seven years as a psychiatrist in private practice, Dr. Saroj Parida. Dr. Parida came to me by way of a referral from a colleague, in the acute aftermath of his having been arrested for insurance fraud for wildly chaotic billing practices involving millions of dollars of inappropriate claims. Although the information he provided to me early in the treatment suggested the possibility of dissociative identity disorder, I leaned strongly toward an alternate diagnosis—bipolar disorder. Why? Let me list the reasons:

1. I would be more comfortable treating a disorder with which I was more familiar, and which would be certainly much easier to treat. ("If all you've got is a hammer, everything's a nail!")
2. A smart sociopath—oh, yes, physicians can be sociopaths too!—could easily fake the symptoms of dissociative identity disorder, hoping to "beat the rap" with an insanity plea.
3. As a "non-expert" in the field of dissociative identity disorder, I wouldn't want to look like a fool hoodwinked into making the diagnosis. The case of Dr. Parida had already made the headlines of all regional newspapers, and I didn't especially care to risk having my name bandied about as the psychiatrist duped into making an outlandish diagnosis.
4. But the most persuasive of reasons was my *doubt* about the diagnosis. I knew that persons who dissociate tend to be highly suggestible—that is, easily convinced about ideas that may not be literally true. What if I inadvertently gave Dr. Parida the suggestion that he had dissociative identity disorder and thereby "induced" the disorder in him? After all, this is a claim often made in the past, and in fact by some in the case of Christine Sizemore mentioned earlier.

Dr. Parida is now in a federal prison for his crimes. He chose to accept full responsibility for them despite his conviction—and mine—that they were committed by dissociated *alters* in a mind conditioned by a traumatic childhood to use dissociation as a means of coping with overwhelming stress. His story is found woven throughout this book. For reasons I will discuss later, I believe that his accepting ultimate responsibility for the conduct of *his* alters has been an indispensable part of his healing.

I managed to stifle my own impulse to dispel my doubt regarding Dr. Parida's diagnosis in favor of the comfort of believing it to be untrue. That is, I gave the "benefit of the doubt" to the diagnosis and treated Dr. Parida for dissociative identity disorder. He gained substantial improvement in his mental health prior to his imprisonment in July 2010, and happily continues to integrate while in prison—a healing that is being accelerated by the continuing expressions of love from his wife and three children. I am convinced that, had I not given the diagnosis the benefit of the doubt, he might no longer be alive to enjoy them. He firmly states this to be true. As we will see later, however, along the way we came across many in the legal profession who did *not* give Dr. Parida—or me—the benefit of the doubt. Fortunately his additional suffering as a consequence has been minimal.

So this book becomes also a story about *doubt* and *belief*, and a cautionary tale about clinging to belief when holding onto doubt is either too scary or too unpopular. In the final analysis, the effectiveness and moral soundness of our approach to persons who dissociate to a harmful extreme—be they patients, neighbors, family members or other loved ones—will not rest upon what we *believe* as much as upon how responsibly we handle our *doubt*. Therefore as you read, you need not trouble yourself by what you find hard to believe, as long as you avoid our very human temptation to cling too much to the comfort of belief and too little to the necessary discomfort of doubt. Enjoy the struggle!

• *1* •

Something for (Almost) Everyone

In a way, the beginning and end of this book are mirror images.

We will start by exploring dissociation as a handy mental vacation from reality that folks in good mental health are able to use in a perfectly healthy way. By the final chapter, we go to the other side of the mirror, where dissociation is the adaptive tool that some psychologically damaged people use to try to feel normal despite horrific aspects of their personal reality.

Just as Lewis Carroll's Alice had intense curiosity about what lay on the other side of the looking glass, as you begin to consider the nature of dissociation and the spectrum of dissociative states—from normal to aberrant—you may find yourself thinking,

> Why, it's turning into a sort of mist now, I declare! It'll be easy enough to get through . . . And certainly the glass WAS beginning to melt away, just like a bright silvery mist. In another moment Alice was through the glass.[1]

TRANCE STATES WE CAN SHARE

Let's start the journey from one side of the mirror to the other with states of dissociation over which most people have some control, that is, those in the realm of normal. Among others, they include the deliberate trance states of hypnosis and meditation and the mind wandering we call *daydreaming*.

Years ago even some more prominent psychiatrists would have considered you to be mentally unstable if you lapsed into occasional daydreams. That's because dissociation means separation; in this case, elements of one's mental life becoming disconnected. The so-called normal state of affairs for the human mind is that consciousness, perception, memory, and a sense of self are integrated. In a state of dissociation, they are not, but it's easy to see how that can happen to varying degrees. We now know that dissociative experiences range from well within the bounds of normal to serious mental illness. Every modern mental health professional I know would therefore defend a daydreamer as normal. In fact, daydreaming fits comfortably into a picture of mental health and may even play a role in achieving high performance.

From the time she was thirteen, my friend Karl's daughter used to daydream about graduating at the top of her class, and she would tell people about it. She'd convinced herself that she would be popular and could go to any college she wanted if she snagged that designation "valedictorian." Four years later, after a lot of homework and a lot of daydreams, she did.

This kind of imagining differs from the *visualization* espoused by many successful competitive athletes—also a type of dissociation. In their "mind's eye" they see themselves doing the sport; they construct a performance scenario and mentally go through the moves needed to win. My friend's daughter didn't envision any of those specifics. She simply daydreamed an accomplishment and experienced the feeling of satisfaction related to it as part of her focused efforts to achieve the goal.

A combined team of psychologists from Stanford University, the University of California, and the University of British Columbia looked at this phenomenon in a study of daydreaming and came to the conclusion that "mind wandering may evoke a unique mental state that may allow otherwise opposing networks to work in cooperation."[2] In other words, their hypothesis is that it can help coordinate the work of neural networks—the wiring circuitry of the brain—that usually function in opposition to each other. So while daydreaming may not give you superpowers, the study suggests it has the potential to kick your mental abilities up a notch, as Emeril would say!

I later had the opportunity to meet my friend's daughter in a professional setting—we decided to coauthor this book—and asked if she would participate in two short exercises to help ascertain her trance capacity. These assessment procedures came out of the remarkable work of the father-son psychiatrist team of Herbert and David Spiegel, coauthors of *Trance and Treatment: Clinical Uses of Hypnosis*.[3] The procedures are relatively simple, but have extraordinary utility in determining how readily a person can experience the therapeutic benefits of hypnosis, an intentional trance state of which most mentally healthy people are capable with minimal training.

The assessment begins with a set of ten questions called the *Structural Cluster Survey*. In the session with Maryann, and basing my questions on those originally designed by the Spiegels, here is what I asked her:

1. When you're in a theater watching a play or a movie, do you ever get so into it that it takes you a few moments to get reoriented after the curtain comes down?

2. As you experience the dimensions of time—past, present, and future—where do you think you focus a greater portion of your attention?

3. A few hundred years ago, a French philosopher and mathematician named Pascal said that it seems as though we have two minds, a heart-mind and a head-mind, and sometimes the two are relative strangers to each other. Which of your two minds has more prominence: your heart-mind or your head-mind?

4. When you are interacting with another person, do you tend to be in control of the interaction, or do you just as easily let the other person be in control if he or she seems to want to be?

5. In terms of your tendency to trust other people in general—not thinking of anyone in particular—where would you place yourself: above average or below average?

6. When you are exposed to a new idea or concept, are you more likely to judge it critically right away, or are you more likely to take it in and then perhaps critically appraise it later on?

7. With regard to your sense of personal responsibility for the things that happen in your life, where would you place yourself: above average or below average?

8. Let's say I tell you there's something new that you can learn and you can learn it equally well by looking at it or by touching it. Which mode of learning would you prefer?

9. There are two parts to a new idea: one part is conceiving of it; the other part is implementing the new idea. Which of the two do you tend to enjoy more—dreaming up new ideas or implementing them?

10. When it comes time to implement a new idea, do you usually follow through by keeping the steps in your head, or are you more likely to write down the steps?

These ten questions help segregate people into categories that correlate very closely with a person's predicted trance capacity. At one end are folks who tend to have a very low trance capacity; the Spiegels refer to them as Apollonian. At the opposite end are persons who tend to have a very high trance capacity; they are referred to as Dionysian. In the middle is the Odyssean group, with a mid-range trance capacity. Their minds are a blend of Apollonian and Dionysian features.

If the names sound familiar, it's because they come from Greek mythology and legend: Apollo, the sun god; Dionysus, the god of wine and revelry; and Odysseus, the Greek king who sneaked his troops past the gates of Troy in the belly of a giant wooden horse.

Successful motivational speakers have a good grasp of the distinguishing behavioral features of the three types, even though they most likely don't use these terms. Anthony Robbins[4] has incorporated trance-related phenomena into his peak-performance workshops, while not utilizing hypnotic trance per se. His use of concepts such as pleasure and pain, and his invitations to "imagine what your life would be like if . . ." would engage the Dionysian and Odyssean types but have less appeal to the Apollonian. At his bidding, the Dionysians and Odysseans may lie on the floor or stand on a chair—something they normally wouldn't do. They know they are there to try to do something positive for themselves, however; they are pumped and ready to work with Robbins, so they are highly motivated to cooperate with him. In contrast to Robbins and his work with general audiences, Jim McCormick[5] has focused on corporate audiences such as executive engineers and people in the financial services industries, where a high percentage of the audience likely falls into the Apollonian category. He relies primarily on logic, not emotion, to reach audiences with a message about the practical value of intelligent risk taking.

While I asked Maryann the above ten questions, I circled an A, O, or D on a sheet of paper to indicate what her answer suggested. For example, she gave a decidedly Apollonian answer to the question about personal responsibility. Since it's the one most influenced by developmental factors, such as values instilled by parents and teachers, it came as no surprise. It was, in fact, her only Apollonian answer—and that told me a great deal about her probable trance capacity. Only three of the responses were Odyssean. For example, in considering the dominance of heart-mind or head-mind, she said that it depended on the circumstances, a typical Odyssean response. With six of the answers falling squarely in the realm of the Dionysian, indications were that she had a mid-to-high trance capacity.

But the questionnaire alone does not confirm trance capacity. It's followed by an exercise developed by the Spiegels called the Hypnotic Induction Profile (HIP) to measure trance capacity on a scale from 0 to 5 and help the subject learn self-hypnosis. The process takes less than ten minutes. As you read through the description of Maryann's experience, keep in mind that a clinician plays an important role in the HIP, so this is not an exercise you would undertake as a party game. I use a script developed by Herbert Spiegel and contained in *Trance and Treatment* throughout the procedure and score responses along the way.

In my office, with gentle ambient light and a solid wood door that blocks sound, Maryann sat in a brown, suede-covered chair. As her body sank into the comfortable furniture, she put her feet on an ottoman, rested her head against the back of the chair, and placed her arms on the cushioned armrests. The process then moved forward with my direction, as follows: After gazing toward me, she looked sharply upward toward her eyebrows, and then continued moving the eyes upward as though she were trying to see the very top of her head. As she continued to look upward, she closed her eyelids very slowly, but all the while, continuing to look upward. She took a deep breath, held it, and then exhaled slowly. She then relaxed her eyes while keeping the lids closed, and at the same time imagined her body floating down through the chair. Concentration on the floating sensation yielded a pleasant and welcoming feeling.

When Maryann seemed completely relaxed, I told her I was going to focus on her left arm and hand and stroke the middle finger of the left hand, which would cause her to develop movement sensations in that finger. I suggested to her that the movements would spread, causing the left hand to feel light and buoyant, and told her to just let it float upward. First one finger, then another, the restless movements would continue, with the elbow bending gently and the forearm floating into an upright position. I told her that her arm would feel like a balloon.

Maryann's hand floated upward, almost carrying the forearm with it the way a helium balloon lifts the string attached to it. I suggested to her that it would remain in that position even after giving the direction to open her eyes, and that when she put it back down at my direction, the arm would float up again, much to her amusement. The final command was that when I touched her left elbow, usual sensation and control would begin to return.

Coming out of trance is essentially a reversal of the ceremony of entering it. The count going into it is a process of asking for one action, then two actions, and then three:

Count of 1: Roll up eyes toward top of head
Count of 1: Slowly close eyes and take a deep breath
Count of 3: Exhale, let eyes relax, and let body float down

So exiting the trance meant that I asked her to "return to the chair," start to focus, and take a breath. After that, I invited her to release the breath, open her eyes, and focus on me.

One important factor in determining the magnitude of Maryann's trance capacity was how long it took her to feel as though her left and right arms had equal sensations. Even after I touched her left elbow to restore control, she reported that her left arm felt much lighter than her right. I told her to make a tight fist a few times until the sensation abated. Finally, she made fists with both hands and raised her arms until there was a sense of balance between the two in terms of weight and control.

Instructions for subsequent self-hypnosis are an integral part of the HIP. Since a trance-prone person likely won't remember the sequence of actions related to the count—I find that people almost never do—I take time afterward to review it so they can do it on their own. The more practice a person gets with the hypnotic induction process, the more readily he or she enters the trance state.

If you identified with the description of relaxing into a hypnotic state, then you've probably experienced it, or something similar to it, like *meditation*. If you didn't, and your thought is "She made it happen!" or "She was faking it!" then I want to offer you this thought: Of course she made it happen; that's not the point. The point is that the person is, in reality, experiencing an altered sensation in the left arm and hand, let alone whether she "made it happen" or not. It is a response to the power of the mind—the ability to dissociate and take suggestions and make them temporarily real. Various studies have looked at what happens in the brain to create a meditative experience. In essence, the location and quantity of brain waves shift and that can be tracked by electroencephalography (EEG). From slow to fast, the waves are known as delta, theta, alpha, and beta, with theta waves most plentiful in the frontal and mid sections of the brain during deep meditation and busier alpha waves going to the rear of the brain.[6] (Delta waves are associated with sleep; beta waves kick in during very task-oriented periods.) Practitioners of self-hypnosis and meditation cause these brain-wave changes to occur by engaging in rituals of breathing, closed eyes, and other de-stressing actions.

The HIP illustrates the three features of hypnotic trance.

1. *Focal awareness* intensified through the induction ceremony
   As a corollary, the process of hypnotic induction involves a temporary reduction of peripheral awareness. An extreme example of this blocking out of peripheral awareness would be the phenomenon of "tunnel vision." The visual field is narrowed, quite literally, despite the absence of any impairment in the eyes or the brain. In that extremely focally absorbed state of mind, peripheral vision is temporarily obliterated. Tunnel vision is an example of dissociation in that visual sensory input to the brain is temporarily disconnected from consciousness.

The eye roll is a physiological measure of focal awareness that correlates very closely with trance capacity. It is scaled on 0 through 4 based upon how much of the sclera, or white of the eye, continues to show as the upper lid closes down over the margin of the iris. (A highly trance-prone person might well get sleepy just reading this.)

2. Experience of *dissociation*

   Physical sensations from the left arm and hand are different from those of the right because of relative temporary disconnection between conscious experience and the usual sensory input from the left arm.

3. Heightened *suggestibility*

   In trance, I give the suggestion that when the person comes out of the trance, and lowers the left arm, it would go right back up again. The speed with which the arm comes back up reflects the subject's degree of suggestibility.

And as I mentioned in explaining why I reiterate the instructions for entering trance, people who can enjoy the trance state experience post-hypnotic amnesia. This gives them a very personal understanding of what happens to someone with an extreme condition like dissociative identity disorder (DID), formerly known as multiple personality disorder. Amnesia typically comes with dissociation. This is why someone with DID like neonatologist Saroj Parida had no recollection that one of his alters perpetrated insurance fraud, or how celebrated Asia expert Robert Oxnam, also a DID sufferer, could deliver a stunning lecture and not know what he said.[7] In Maryann's case, I told her that when I touched her left elbow, control would begin to return to normal. But when I asked her later if she recalled anything I said that could account for the sensations returning to normal, she didn't remember it.

Here's another provocative factor that, again, gives some insight into what people who have dissociation-related mental illness can discover in therapy. Maryann did remember what I told her about touching her left elbow when I reminded her of it. That's another feature of trance: You don't lose your memory trace for things that happen in trance. It just means that without some kind of contextual cue, you are not likely to remember. The phenomenon is similar to the way a person has blackouts when drunk, but still stores memories during those blackouts. If the person gets drunk again, he's more likely to remember what happened in his previous drunken state.

This is called *state-dependent memory*, and a good example of it is the case of a woman named Jan, who routinely did her homework in college while she was high on marijuana. As part of her rite of passage for graduation, she had to take a comprehensive examination in her major; she failed it twice. Finally, a therapist she had gone to see recommended that she take the exam "stoned" since she always studied under the influence of pot. She did so and passed. One of the many studies documenting the occurrence of this phenomenon was done by psychologist James Eric Eich, who offers the following conclusion: "The finding of principal interest is that access to or retrieval of information about the target items is impaired when the subject's pharmacological state is changed between the study and test sessions of the experiment, in comparison with conditions in which his or her state remains the same on both occasions."[8]

This is illustrative of an issue with dissociative disorders, as we will see later. The amnesia that the person has does not mean he's lost the memory trace entirely. There are highly specific contextual cues or circumstances that are going to be necessary in order to retrieve the memories. Through questions and conversation in sessions with our patients, therapists try to discover such cues so that memories stored while the patient was in a dissociated state can surface.

In summary, many people with no signs of mental illness, but with some capacity for experiencing trance states, know what it's like to dissociate: We daydream, visualize, allow therapists to guide us into hypnotic states, self-hypnotize, or plunge into a meditation, all of which entail our temporarily feeling disconnected—dissociated—from usual sensory input.

THE UTILITY OF TRANCE

Trance has many uses, including the routine ways that trances help us to sleep better, remove ourselves from tension, enhance therapy with a psychologist or psychiatrist, and almost limitlessly more. As I suggested in the story of Maryann daydreaming about graduating as valedictorian, trance can have a function in life that is more than mitigating or solving a problem; it can also be part of a program to realize human potential.

The purpose of teaching self-hypnotic trance, without using the trance state to address a particular physical or psychological issue, is to enable one to develop a talent and put it to work at will. It's a little like physical exercise. The person doesn't necessarily want to participate in a particular sport, but it's a good idea to exercise anyway. In short, a person with a substantial trance capacity should try to cultivate it because it will come in handy in a lot of activities of daily living. For example, a person with good trance capacity who enjoys meditation can train himself to enjoy a radically enhanced meditative state by using a formal trance induction. People who want to fall asleep more efficiently can use a specific kind of trance imagery to facilitate sleep. I've done that a number of times myself using "the screen." (Like the HIP itself, the screen idea is one of the many practical applications advocated by the Spiegels.)

I visualize either a blue sky or a movie screen about fifteen or twenty feet away. Onto the screen, I project the thoughts that keep jarring me awake. The thoughts on the screen are not gone from my mind; they are just way out there, and getting further and further away.

A commonly heard complaint is that people say they can't sleep because their mind is "racing a mile a minute." One intuitive suggestion is to think of nothing. But if you think of nothing then you are thinking hard about thinking about nothing. Instead, project those thoughts on the screen to distance them, if not remove them, from consciousness.

While the screen captures the disruptive thoughts, float down through the mattress in the same manner that I tell people in the hypnotic induction ceremony to float down into the chair. The sensation of floating almost obligatorily relaxes the body by enhancing the functioning of the parasympathetic nervous system, which is that branch of the autonomic nervous system responsible for resting functions of the body like digestion and heart beat. Its counterpart, the sympathetic nervous system, is responsible for the fight-flight-freeze response. The problem that a lot of people have in not being able to fall asleep is that the sympathetic nervous system is in overdrive. For the body to relax or function appropriately, there has to be a constant dynamic balance between the activities undertaken by the sympathetic and parasympathetic nervous systems.

In a situation like this, with a trance exercise inducing a quick parasympathetic reaction, it's easy to see how hypnotic trance can be very useful for people even though they might not have any particular pathological problem to work on, such as anxiety or a phobia.

Not long ago, a man came to me with the specific request that we try to use hypnosis to address his high blood pressure. He had been referred to me by his cardiologist after he told the doctor that he didn't want to use medicine to control the problem. The patient was a bright and successful businessman whom I would describe as psychologically minded—really in tune with his mental potential.

I asked him questions about his condition as well as a few more to determine how pure his motivation was to bring his blood pressure down, such as "Why do you want your blood pressure to go down?" Motivation is a very important factor in trance. If you have a high trance capacity but are not highly motivated, then the hypnosis probably won't support the desired result. The happy outcome is that he succeeded in developing the self-hypnosis techniques he needed to keep his blood pressure in check without medicine. Surely enough, this man found one feature of hypnosis especially helpful for him: paradox! We can't *really* float down through a chair—but we feel we are. This man "got" the paradox that one of the best things he could do to lower his blood pressure is to let go of his preoccupation with lowering his blood pressure. He could then use self-hypnosis to practice and intensify that letting go.

With the exception of those rare individuals with extremely high trance potential, people won't do something within trance that they really don't want to do. So in a nightclub act, the hypnotist recruits people from the audience. Those willing to participate are motivated to become part of the show, just as participants in an Anthony Robbins workshop are motivated to let him help them achieve peak performance. Almost invariably the volunteers from the audience are trance-prone people; they have a theatrical bent to them. But if the hypnotist gives them a suggestion that goes counter to their morality—like "take off all your clothes"—they won't do it. The motivational state must be intense, and it must be consistent with the person's conscience. So people who make complete fools of themselves don't mind making complete fools of themselves; there is no dissonance between making fools of themselves and their conscience or social sense. Similarly, a therapist can't "make" a patient lower his blood pressure through hypnosis unless the patient wants to do it.

I have already asserted that Maryann's assessment results indicated that she has a relatively high trance capacity, so it should come as no surprise that she was a good subject for hypnosis involving an unusual challenge. In the mid-1980s, she had developed a strong rapport with a particular hypnotherapist in the course of doing articles about the uses of hypnosis for smoking cessation, pain mitigation, and performance improvement in sports—some of which were personal interests she pursued with him. In 1987, she was scheduled for facial surgery and decided she would like to try to use post-hypnotic suggestions in lieu of anesthesia since she had had positive experiences with hypnosis before. The surgeon, Dr. Harvey Austin, was familiar with the hypnotherapist's work and agreed to perform the surgery without the use of the usual anesthetics—although he had them nearby just in case something went awry. Dr. Austin then proceeded to perform a lip lift on Maryann as she used her trance capacity to mitigate pain and bleeding. She actually watched the entire procedure, a surgery pioneered by Dr. Austin that involved excising an ellipse of tissue from below the nose to raise the lip slightly, thereby exposing more of her smile. The post-hypnotic suggestions were things like "the surgeon's touch is very soothing" and the notion that she would feel pressure from the scalpel, but no pain.

A child's trance capacity can support mental health and reduce stress in her life by enabling her to escape briefly and harmlessly to a make-believe world. When little Janie fought with her mother, she would lock herself in her room with her dolls. Her mother was not at all an abusive woman; in fact, she was a wonderful, loving mother making necessary efforts to discipline her contrarian daughter. Janie had good food to eat and a safe home, but she felt threatened very easily by her mother's somewhat stern tone. Locking herself in her room made her feel safe and, her need for safety met, she would proceed to "bond" with her dolls until she settled down and restored her awareness of the strong bond she had with mother.

Janie had a healthy approach to conflict without even realizing it. She felt rage at her mother for disciplining her, but she loved her intensely. What could she do with that rage? Talk to her dolls. Take a different child without Janie's ability to use her imagination to fulfill an immediate need and you could have someone feeling starved for affection, even though the love was right in front of her.

To have a flight of fancy—to experience trance—you need to respond to the power of suggestion. It's as though the dolls were more than cloth and rubber assemblies to Janie; they were little people. For a few moments, Janie's dolls became her family of choice. They had life for a little while and enabled her to work out her frustrations and maybe discover new options in relating to her mother. The chit-chat with her room of "little girls" gave her insights about how to talk to her mother and how to respond. Problems that seemed huge to a seven-year-old got worked out through role playing.

Janie's capability for dissociation helped her grow up happy and contributed to a healthy relationship with her mother. But if she were a child with a low capacity for suggestibility (as, for example, do most children with attention deficit hyperactivity disorder [ADHD]), the mother-daughter conflict would have played out much differently. The ADHD child is at a terrible disadvantage. Instead of locking herself in her room with her dolls, the ADHD child is more likely to run out the door, grab her bike out of the garage, and career down the sidewalk while spitting invectives.

While many video games seem perfectly harmless, some seem to me to be exploitative of children and adults with the high stimulus craving of persons with ADHD. The video game is intense and constantly changing stimulation. It delivers rapid reward so that the player doesn't get too frustrated. It doesn't permit boredom. The risk is that it may not help develop the child's own mind as a tool of entertainment in the way that Janie's dolls served that purpose.

The utility of trance states that people choose, or at least can choose not to enter, should be clear from these examples. There are also many complementary examples such as trance states that enhance athletic performance, eradicate phobias and bad habits, and much more. Even if you acknowledge the value of them, however, there is no guarantee that you can take advantage of trance states.

WHEN TRANCE IS MISSING

Some kids sit in math class bored to tears. Hard to imagine, but it happens! A high-trance-capacity person like Ginny might lapse into a daydream about Justin Bieber while the teacher runs through quadratic equations. Across the aisle from her is Tom, a person with a low dissociative capacity who handles that boredom by throwing spitballs at Ginny. In other words, while Ginny recruits something from her internal environment to alleviate her boredom, Tom recruits something from the external environment. People with ADHD will be among those who pester the kid across the aisle or secretly play video games in the back of the room rather than daydream. The predisposition toward one approach or the other belongs to the individual's innate set of characteristics, like eye color or height.

A problem I see a lot in young patients is something I call *existential boredom*. My patients with short attention span who are easily distracted—not necessarily those with an organic problem like ADHD, but often they do have it—require an inordinate amount of external stimulation in order to keep them internally calm and to keep them interested in the world around them. They tend to be very much defined by what they do. They are not reflective people. They are not people blessed with imagination. They are not people very capable of dissociation, so they can't entertain themselves with daydreams. As a result, they are utterly dependent on their environment and need something to do in order to relieve themselves from what would be an acute and painful state of existential boredom. That is, suddenly their life has no meaning and the world has no value for them. If you are in the presence of someone who faces that crisis, you can feel it. When I sense it, I know that something urgent has to be done.

Some time ago I saw Craig, a twenty-year-old man. He had just been discharged from his fourth drug rehabilitation within a year and launched his first session by announcing, "Whatever it is that's going to help me, I know it isn't another rehab." When I did a careful evaluation of him, I learned two things. First of all, he has an anxiety problem, and his social anxiety problem has deprived him of a number of activities that would have been highly stimulating and rewarding and given him far greater self-esteem. He was an excellent athlete, but by the time he was a junior in high school, his social anxiety was so bad that he could not appear in front of people anymore. But he didn't know he had a social anxiety; he didn't know what held him back. Narcotic drug abuse took him away from his problem.

Craig has a temperament that causes him to crave an inordinate amount of stimulation from his environment. He is incapable of entertaining himself through reflection or daydreaming. He dropped out of college, despite his aptitudes, because he had never satisfactorily identified the purpose of college for him and had virtually no interest in studying anything.

To compound his existential boredom, he felt isolation and loneliness when his girlfriend broke up with him. When I met with him right after that occurred, his desperation was palpable. "What can I do?" he begged.

"Was there *ever* a time your life when you got excited about something you might like to do with your life?"

He gave an embarrassed smile. "Yeah, "I thought I'd like to be a pilot." And then he added, "A military pilot."

"The military is probably unrealistic for you with your drug history," I told him gently, "but I know of nothing that would necessarily keep you from pursuing a pilot's license." That didn't get much response from him. He knew that commercial pilots don't zip around and shoot things. As exciting as many of us would think it would be to get a private pilot's license or to have responsibility for a jet aircraft like a commercial pilot, in his mind, there wasn't enough potential for the level of stimulation he required.

I persisted. "Maybe you want to start taking flight lessons and see what happens. Why not make a deal with your parents so that if you get a job and keep it, they might go halvsies with you on your lessons?" He showed a little spark, but not a lot.

And then I told him a story I'd read about fifteen years prior about a glider pilot. An airplane towed him above the skies of Pennsylvania and the pilot took his glider all the way to Tennessee, turned around and glided all the way back to Pennsylvania without touching the ground.

Craig beamed and leaned forward: "How did he do that?" And with that question, I saw more animation and hope in his face than ever before. The more I told him about gliders riding thermals, the more excited he got. He left that day with a bounce in his step.

The experience with Craig made me wonder again, as I had wondered often before, if someone temperamentally like him could learn to daydream, to get absorbed in a fanciful notion just long enough to get a glimpse of himself in the cockpit of an aircraft. For those of us who have that capacity, we can't imagine not having it. The flip side is Craig's mental world, where that kind of mind wandering rarely if ever happens.

Just as our capacity to experience trance affects the way we handle the dreariness of life, it also affects the way we handle life's stresses. Our defensive operations, that is, our natural response to the stresses, also divide us into those who dissociate and those who find other means of coping. If a person experiences traumatic life stresses, the person with the high dissociative potential may well experience dissociative types of mental illness in the aftermath. Subsequent chapters categorize and describe what those illnesses are, the most extreme of which is dissociative identity disorder. In contrast, the person not trance-prone may act out or become severely depressed or anxiety ridden.

The case of Mary Bell, who committed murders of other children when she was only ten and eleven years old, illustrates in a horrible and extreme way how a victim of trauma with no dissociative capacity might act out. Mary Bell's prostitute mother had apparently involved the child in her sadistic sexual encounters with her johns, among other abusive and neglectful acts. Mary's retaliation involved fatally harming those she could, that is, two little boys who could not stand up to her. Mary Bell's frightening, sociopathic behavior arouses a question seeded with irony: Would the capacity to dissociate, even to the point of having the mind fracture into multiple personalities, have potentially given Mary a chance for a more normal life than the one she had—and prevented the loss of the other children's lives?[9]

A less dramatic, but no less salient example of what low trance capacity can lead to, surfaced with Sally, one of my patients whose mother was a German "war bride" after World War II. Throughout Sally's childhood she experienced her mother as wildly unpredictable in mood and frequently emotionally abusive to her, leaving Sally with severe deficits in self-esteem and in her ability to trust others. As she gained traction against these deficits in therapy and started to initiate conversations with her mother as one adult woman to another, her mother remarkably began to tell her stories for the first time ever about growing up in Nazi Germany. She recalled that, when she was in grade school, SS troops[10] would come in for indoctrination lectures. They either terrified the children while inspiring them to daydream about an invincible Third Reich, or simply terrified them. These abrupt, frightening experiences were traumatizing for my patient's mother, a woman with almost certainly low trance capacity who couldn't swallow the propaganda like the more suggestible, highly trance-prone child. She didn't have dissociative defenses to utilize, and therefore avoided indoctrination (the good news) at the expense of a sort of paranoid wariness of people in general (the bad news). We know that trauma can pass down through generations in many ways. This example illustrates that the dissociative capacity of the sufferer will affect the specific form that the transmission takes.

Stories like that of Mary Bell and Sally's mother raise the question, just what percentage of a population has a high trance capacity? As you travel around the world and visit different cultures, different communities, and different families, that number could change quite a bit. In fact, the phenomenon of an entire community or nation being essentially mesmerized by a leader is a subject for another book. If you look solely at statistics related to post-traumatic stress disorder (PTSD) sufferers to get a sense of what portion of the population has a high trance capacity, here's a well-researched number: According to the Sidran Traumatic Stress Institute, "an estimated 70 percent of adults in the United States have experienced a traumatic event at least once in their lives and up to 20 percent of these people go on to develop PTSD."[11] The clinical symptoms of PTSD include dissociation, amnesia, and flashbacks (a kind of trance), all of which depend on reasonably high trance capacity on the part of the person.

THE NEUROBIOLOGY OF TRANCE

In psychiatry, technology brought a pre-dawn light in the late twentieth century. Studies starting in the 1990s using functional magnetic resonance imaging (fMRI) began looking at blood flow in the brain and mapping brain structures so that we could get some picture of how certain activities—daydreaming, for example—corresponded to physiological events. In the twenty-first century, fMRI has helped give us tiny glimmers of daylight, but we have a way to go until we see exact correlations between specific areas of the brain and specific behaviors. fMRI has proven to be a worthy partner to behavioral and electroencephalography (EEG) measurements in studies of mental processes; the downside is that interpretation of the images presents complicated challenges. For one thing, the mere discovery of a relationship between a piece of behavior and an image of particular neural activity doesn't necessary mean there's a direct causal link. The kind of direct connection that an EEG can demonstrate between relaxation techniques and location and quantity of brain waves is not what we usually find in these studies.

That said, of the different centers for various conscious functions that are being identified in fMRI-related studies, two in particular are of interest in the discussion of dissociation: the attention associational area and the orientation associational area.

A big difference between sleep and anesthesia on the one hand and trance on the other hand is the attention associational area, which in sleep is shut down, but in trance is enhanced. There's more activity going on than usual. The mind wandering study referenced at the beginning of the chapter gets to the heart of that difference.

Regarding the orientation associational area, some people in transcendental experiences refer to an "oceanic feeling" in which they don't perceive any boundaries between themselves and their environment. Dr. Andrew Newberg, a radiologist at the University of Pennsylvania Hospital, has done elegant brain-imaging studies on people like praying nuns and meditating monks.[12] He has demonstrated that, at the peak of the meditative experience, the right parietal region (behind the ear) does not appear to function at all—that there's no input to it whatsoever. In normal consciousness, this area of the brain does two things: (1) it gives us our sense of orientation in space; (2) it gives us an awareness of our physical boundaries, where we end and where the rest of the universe begins. If there's no input or output from that area, the person can have an experience of oneness with the rest of the universe. The temporary lack of perceived boundary is a kind of dissociation. It's an intentional state of shutdown produced by the person meditating—not the result of accident or illness, but a deliberate act. The brain verifies what the person intends, just as Michael Jordan's body would verify his intention to make a jump shot by putting certain muscles to work.

In the upcoming chapters, I describe dissociation as something other than a conscious decision, even though some part of the traumatized individual's brain does "choose" dissociation as a way of coping with an awful experience or repeated traumas. It is also not something that the person can choose to abandon readily; there is no "Gee, I think I'll not do that again," and then the dissociation suddenly stops. As you read, you may well recognize some of the descriptions from your own personal experience. It's highly likely you will feel as though you have something in common with people who dissociate involuntarily, or that you have friends and relatives who have described similar experiences.

· 2 ·

Entering the Land of the Lost

An association of engineers hired a friend of mine to provide the after-dinner speech at their annual conference. Two hours prior to the scheduled presentation time, she learned that the location had been changed to a room with a different configuration such that she would not be able to use her slides. And during the sound check, the battery pack for her wireless microphone fell apart and had to be duct-taped together. Over and over again, she told herself, "No problem. I'm a professional."

By all reports, her speech pleased the crowd of 150 engineers and spouses. But she knew she had not reached her customary level of performance. During the presentation, she saw herself on stage, as if she were standing behind the self-assured woman in black evening pants, a purple silk jacket, and black high heels. She looked at the properly animated body, feet shoulder-width apart, gesturing openly to the audience. As the words of the speech came out of her mouth, her mind fleetingly focused on the fact that she seemed robotic.

Did this dissociation result in trauma, causing her to never again set foot on a stage? No. The speech she saw as a failure was not a traumatic experience—upsetting, yes, but not traumatic. Nonetheless, that moment of dissociation is the only thing she remembers about being on stage that night.

Without question, my friend did not choose to dissociate, nor could she choose not to. The memory of it makes her feel regretful and uncomfortable, but it never undermines her planning and confidence as she heads for another stage and another audience. The same experience might have left a scar on an amateur's mind, causing that person to revisit the scene, and perhaps even triggering fear of ever doing another presentation. This cycle does not get activated

23

in a professional whose mind has been trained to override the negative memory by putting it in the context of a very positive career.

Hers is a type of dissociative experience that many mentally healthy people have shared, but it suggests (more than a pleasant daydream does) how an unpleasant moment can trigger dissociation. During the eight-week run of a show, actors performing six nights and two afternoons a week will probably report the same kind of experience at least once during the run—maybe the Wednesday afternoon they felt "off." Or you might be driving your car late on a rainy night in Pittsburgh and nearly hit a pedestrian in a black raincoat. Everyone comes away unscathed, but you replay the "memory" of seeing yourself stop short and facing the anger and shock of the pedestrian.

These experiences do not suggest that a personality has fractured, meaning that the core personality is temporarily replaced by another as is the case with DID. All of the above situations involve a dissociated "state of self" in the role of observer. In a sense, the person steps out of himself to witness the uncomfortable event in a dispassionate way.

Chris Costner Sizemore describes analogous experiences that occurred in her childhood in *I'm Eve*,[1] the book that documents her life with multiple personalities, which was also covered in the movie and book *The Three Faces of Eve*. One of the first such experiences was when little Christine saw another red-headed girl who looked just like her watch calmly as her father helped pull a deceased neighbor out of an irrigation ditch.

While people with mental illness might dissociate as a result of a negative experience, they certainly aren't the only ones. The difference is that mentally healthy people remain intact; that is, they do not go on to dissociate repeatedly at times and in ways that significantly interfere with their functioning. With that thought in mind, when does dissociation mean that a person has a psychological problem?

WHEN DISSOCIATION MEANS MENTAL ILLNESS

According to the current edition of the *Diagnostic and Statistical Manual of Mental Disorders* (DSM-IV, or simply DSM),[2] mental illness is defined by the damage it does both outside and inside one's life. Although the DSM is sometimes justly criticized by some of my colleagues, one very remarkable key principle emphasized in the manual is the delineation of what is required in order to declare a diagnosis. Namely, there has to be significant impairment in either social or occupational functioning, or both; and/or there has to be substantial subjective distress, meaning distress within the person. If there is no significant internal distress because of the symptoms, and there is no impairment in social or occupational functioning, then there is no disorder. The person might be unusual or odd, but a clinician should not label him mentally ill—according to the DSM.

Let's briefly look at how the DSM's value is substantial but limited at the same time. In child psychiatry there are several disorders on the autism spectrum. On the mild end is Asperger's syndrome. A child may have no impairment related to school or social activities, and no distress—except the distress of being told she has Asperger's syndrome. According to the DSM, my friend Jack's daughter does not have a disorder, even though her pediatrician rendered a diagnosis of Asperger's, suggested by the fact that she seemed lacking in social skills and was very clumsy as a little girl. Ultimately, she excelled in many school subjects, performed in plays throughout high school and college, and now has a long-term boyfriend. Jack and his wife innocuously worked therapy into their daughter's routine, such as activities designed to help her read body language better, but never told their daughter about the diagnosis. As a result, she never faced the burden of feeling different or "less than." I believe the pediatrician made the mistake of diagnosing the girl with a disorder in the absence of any persistent impairment in social or occupational functioning or internal distress (e.g., anxiety or self-esteem problems). In other words, "nerdiness" or quirkiness and clumsiness are not indicative of a mental illness.

The mistake is made from both ends of the diagnostic effort, that is, the clinician and the individual. Clinicians make the mistake of diagnosing when there is no disorder, and individuals make the mistake of overestimating the role an identified disorder plays in their lives. It has become all too common for people to excuse their poor performance with, "Oh, it's my ADD kicking in again" or "I'm so phobic about that." In some instances, this leads to unnecessary or inappropriate treatment.

In contrast, people suffering from the most extreme type of dissociative disorder, DID, may be so high functioning that they—and people around them—tend to underplay periods of amnesia and erratic behavior. Even though Saroj Parida functioned brilliantly as a neonatologist, other medical professionals around him knew that he sometimes couldn't remember where to park his car and would suddenly have no recollection of certain people that he'd seen repeatedly. Instead of urging him into therapy, colleagues dismissed the gaps. Their rationale: "Saroj is just an annoying, eccentric, egocentric genius." In DSM terms, they didn't consider him to have any impairment or distress.

When one of his alters launched a campaign to get Saroj help by perpetrating insurance fraud, this other personality took action that explicitly suggested impairment. Based on Saroj's lauded performance at work, standing in the community, and financial success, he had no reason to commit such a crime—except to force himself into a situation where he would receive psychiatric help.

Partly because of my work with Saroj, I have begun to use an expanded diagnostic approach by combining DSM-IV with a novel diagnostic system, the *Psychodynamic Diagnostic Manual* (PDM).[3] This modified system includes the DSM-IV diagnosis as one of three axes, the other two of which are personality structure and mental functioning. DSM-IV provides the symptomatic picture, but then for each patient, I generate a personality profile as well as a mental functioning profile. The latter is a broad range of features including learning style, learning disabilities, relationship and attachment style, reflective functioning, and other factors covered in the PDM.

The reason the PDM took shape is that many psychoanalytic therapists wanted to contribute to a much more broad-based and meaningful diagnostic formulation for each patient. Combining the approach with the DSM offers a more comprehensive picture than the DSM alone, since we want to look at the whole person in diagnosing a mental illness. In fall 2011, I began incorporating this new diagnostic approach into my evaluations and into the treatment plans of the students at three in-school, partial hospital programs for which I provide psychiatric services.

For example, the concept of temperament is accounted for in the PDM but not per se in the DSM. Two pioneer child psychiatrists named Alexander Thomas and Stella Chess led the New York Longitudinal Study of Temperament, in which they followed babies into adult life.[4] They kept assiduous records of the subjects and distilled nine categories of temperament from the data, that is, inborn behavioral predispositions that remained relatively unchanged into adult life. Therein sits the distinction between temperament and personality. Personality arises from the intersection of temperament, intellectual and physical endowment, and environmental influences that the person experiences throughout the formative years of life.

Stella Chess came to Penn State University's Hershey Medical Center campus as a visiting professor during my residency there. One of the illustrations she gave on the importance of parents understanding temperament is the story of a little girl who had a difficult temperament. She was emotionally intense and very sensitive. She had a predominantly gloomy mood and, as part of that, was fussy, irritable, and argumentative. Her mother got along with her relatively well, but her father did not. In fact, he couldn't stand her. By the time she was five years old, she became anxiety ridden because of the conflict with her father. She came into treatment with Chess, who saw what was going on and empathically interpreted the temperamental mismatch between the little girl and her father. Going away with a deeper understanding of their child's nature, the parents tempered responses to her and, in general, the home situation improved and remained tolerable for several years. Her parents brought the child back when she was nine years old with the same story: conflict with the father. Chess took them back into treatment. In the midst of this second treatment, it came time in school for the students to learn their first musical instrument. For whatever reason, the little girl chose the violin as her instrument and, within months, her teacher and parents recognized that she had a rare gift. She advanced rapidly and quickly became a virtuoso. Suddenly her anxiety cleared up and her relationship with her father transformed, so much so that the positive development confounded Chess. She expressed her puzzlement to the father, noting that the child's temperament hadn't changed a bit. She was still intense, sensitive, and argumentative at times. He explained that he finally realized that those features of his daughter are simply her "artistic temperament." So what he had been identifying as pathological all along suddenly became part of a gift. To him, her behavior could now be seen as admirable rather than annoying or sick: "That's how artists are!"

What if there had been no music classes in school, or the father had no appreciation for music and continued to judge his daughter as abnormal? What if the parents had taken her to a different mental health professional— one who excluded temperament from the set of diagnostic factors? The little girl might have earned a label "disturbed" and been put on a medication to smooth her moods. The result could have been a child who abandoned music and wondered why she even ended up on this earth.

Here again, the opposite can occur, with a child living in apparent harmony with his parents, all the while struggling with grave psychological conflicts. Perhaps a professional evaluating a young Saroj Parida with more than just " behavioral impairment" in mind would have seen his extraordinary trance ability and irregularities in sleep and response to certain stimuli as indications that it was time to dig deeper—to find out why young Saroj acted a little differently on occasion.

On the surface, Saroj's early story suggests he should have been jumping for joy all the time, instead of having a tendency to be withdrawn and even sullen in social circumstances. At an early age, his academic accomplishments distinguished him. For example,

- In 1972, he was awarded the National Science Talent Scholarship and ranked ninth in the country.
- When he was twelve, Saroj was picked as the youngest school student to represent his state at a national science convention held in New

Delhi. Only two students were picked from each state to assemble in the capital and meet the then–prime minister, Indira Gandhi.
• At the age of fifteen, he entered a top-notch medical school, where the odds of anyone getting in are astronomically low.

Even then, he didn't do it alone; his alters started to take shape to "help" him adapt to difficult situations. His parents had no knowledge of the sexual abuse he'd endured from the houseboy, and his emerging team of personalities would try to ensure that they would never find out—and he could forget. They also helped him cover up the fact that he felt like a misfit in school, and later at work. In recalling his life before integration, he wrote, "Imagine that almost my entire life was devoid of normal human emotions to a great extent and that my social toolbox was empty. It seems I lived my entire life in a fog."

Saroj's case illustrates perfectly when dissociation means mental illness. His mind had no choice except to dissociate, in that his enormous capacity to dissociate under stress was inborn, like temperament is inborn. His mind grappled with a paradox: For Saroj to feel normal, or unified, and to appear normal on the outside, he had to become abnormal, or divided, on the inside. With someone like Saroj, taking a slice of his highly productive day and analyzing it in terms of symptoms alone would yield nothing that strongly suggests a disorder as severe as dissociative identity disorder—or even something more minor. Until his alters became saliently apparent when he was in his late forties, the only way someone schooled in the mind might have concluded that there was a serious problem was by looking at the whole person.

DISORDERS THAT DANCE WITH DISSOCIATION

A brief look at the commonalities and differences between dissociative disorders and the more familiar conditions of bipolar and post-traumatic stress disorders will help illuminate how clinicians can make a wrong diagnosis.

On a summer afternoon in 1992, Emily and her husband Robert exited a Beechcraft Twin Bonanza with four other skydivers over the trees and homes of rural Virginia. The six came together in the air and created multiple formations before they separated and deployed their parachutes. Five of the jumpers landed at the drop zone, a clearing in a heavily wooded area where the air strip and hanger were located. While under canopy, Robert had spotted a large picnic going on in the residential area just beyond the trees surrounding the drop zone. Children played softball; smoke rose from the grills filled with chicken and burgers. "They would love it if I landed in their yard!"

Robert concluded. He made an abrupt turn toward the yard and swooped in over the children, over the grill, over the picnic tables—landing perfectly. In his black jump suit, black parachute, and black rig, Robert flew in with the persona of Batman, which is what the kids yelled as he approached the ground. Everyone applauded and one of the adults volunteered to drive Robert back to the drop zone, where his wife and buddies paced anxiously. The drop zone owner concealed his rage while the neighbor was there, but knew that he could have been shut down for this "bandit demo," that is, a demonstrative skydive he didn't have permission to do from anyone who mattered, like the Federal Aviation Administration, United States Parachute Association, and the people who owned the house where he jumped. Had one thing gone wrong or the neighbors complained that this was an intrusion rather than welcome entertainment, the Beechcraft would have been grounded for skydiving purposes.

Robert has bipolar disorder, and his state that day was manic; he enjoyed a sense of grandiosity. Mark Whitacre, the person Matt Damon portrayed in *The Informant!*, was in a manic state when he committed the financial crimes that put him in prison. The person in a manic state might feel so unrealistically empowered that he can do anything and not have to suffer the consequences of it. When Robert eyed the landing site among myriad obstacles, some of which were human and in motion, he felt like Batman. He had the confidence of Batman and firmly believed he had the skills.

Just like Mark Whitacre, Robert did in fact have higher-than-normal skills that enabled him to pull off the challenging feat. As displayed in this landing, Robert's canopy control skills might even be compared with Mark's intellectual genius. Nevertheless, his stunt was irrationally foolish.

A person in a manic state might even feel so grandiose that he concludes, "Because I want to do it, that makes it right." So the grandiosity of believing an outlandish feat is possible combines with the conviction there are no negative consequences and the assumption that, just because he thought of it, it's okay to do it.

What are the commonalities such bipolar bandits have with Saroj in the days leading up to, as well as immediately after, he filed fraudulent insurance claims? Let's just look at Mark and Saroj for a moment. Both committed a nonviolent crime while in a radically altered state of mind, wherein the agency of conscience and morality was temporarily disabled. Both had the potential to hide from suspicion longer than most because of their prior work and reputations. Both had no financial need for the money they stole. Both are geniuses, so even after getting caught, the first assumption of the law enforcement and legal communities would be that they were smart enough to fake a mental illness.

Another commonality: The unaffected state in both of the men knew right from wrong and had a fundamentally sound conscience, but in the pathological state—Saroj in the dissociated state and Mark Whitacre in the manic state—their behavior belied their core healthy conscience. And even in their altered states, neither one had violent tendencies toward others, although they had to the potential to harm themselves. Both contemplated suicide.

Where they differ is in the dimension of dissociation. The bipolar person is not dissociated. Mark's altered state had to do with a radical elevation of mood—so enormously elevated that, for various reasons, it disabled his conscience. None of his experiences involved dissociation in the amnestic sense at all, such as what Saroj experienced.

Saroj remembers when he first found out about his crimes. On February 26, 2009, the authorities paid a visit to his elegant home in central Pennsylvania. He recalls: "A car pulled up on my driveway. Two gentlemen in long black overcoats jumped out of the car and rushed to my front door. I was sitting in my study, as though I had not moved from that chair in years. They rang the bell and I opened the door. My wife happened to be in the house at that time and accompanied me to the door. These two gentlemen identified themselves as 'agents' and asked us if there was anybody else in the house and whether we had any weapons. We said 'no.' They said that they came from the Attorney General's office and the federal government. We were bewildered."

Unlike in bipolar disorder, dissociation is almost routinely a part of PTSD, but the latter is classified as an anxiety disorder rather than a dissociative one. Those with PTSD suffer dissociative-like phenomena, specifically intrusive recollections wherein the past will become the present. Psychiatrist David Spiegel, the Stanford professor of psychiatry and behavioral science referenced previously as the coauthor of *Trance and Treatment*, has worked extensively with veterans suffering from PTSD. At a training I attended years ago, he remarked that he found when going through the chronic wards at the Veterans Administration hospital in Palo Alto, California, that a good number of the men housed there who were diagnosed with schizophrenia did not in fact have schizophrenia. Rather, they had PTSD with dissociation, and the dissociated states were mistaken for psychotic states.

To highlight the difference between a dissociated state and the kind of disconnection from reality experienced by someone in a psychotic state, I offer a paragraph from an unpublished autobiographical work provided to us by convicted murderer Ward Yont. Ward is serving a life sentence for his crimes, but now has a connection to reality and to his destructive behavior that was completely missing while in his psychotic states:

If my theories were correct, then engineered into the ceiling-panels was a highly advanced mind-scanning device that was triggered by ultra-sensitive, voice-activated switches. I'd suspected all of this before I went into the store, which is why I said nothing until I was first spoken to. If you'll recall, he said, "May I help you?" It's a simple enough question, really, for any layperson shopping for say, *a pair of shoes,* perhaps. But, to the keen intellect of a select few, (and I'm definitely one of them), this harmless interrogative might've flipped the switches to a device whose technology was decades ahead of its time—possibly inducing any agenda at all into the mind of whomever should find himself standing in the induction zone. Only when I walked into the store did it occur to me that the induction zone at this particular facility must've been located in the shoe department.[5]

Ward's delusions did not make him a "different person" in the same way that Saroj Parida's alters caused him to behave like an infant or raging protector. He did not dissociate; he instead suffered a false, paranoid version of reality. He didn't have a picture-perfect childhood, but Ward's mental health issues and those of persons with similar mental illnesses are believed to have a substantial genetic component rather than being rooted in repeated trauma.

Victims of trauma who, unlike Saroj, are not predisposed to trance have coping mechanisms that do not involve dissociation. As I mentioned in chapter 1 in the section called "When Trance Is Missing," some victims of trauma will act out, others have depression, and others may express anxiety in more idiosyncratic ways. And then there are those who, because of amazing resilience and great environmental support, seem to have no symptoms.

TRUE DISSOCIATIVE DISORDERS

It is useful to think of mental illnesses as a person's effort to adapt—however ineffectively—to the stresses of life. Dissociative disorders are an effort at adaptation by walling off painful memories or feelings from consciousness. In brief, the dissociative disorders currently recognized by the DSM are these:

Dissociative identity disorder (DID). The person partially fractures mentally into different people in a way, but may well maintain the ability to do surgery, practice law, run a company—anything. Dr. Martha Stout references one fascinating case in her insightful work *The Myth of Sanity,*[6] in which a DID-affected mother consistently showed motherly abilities and priorities regardless of whether she was in the persona of a five-year-old child, a vicious self-injurer, or her normal self.

In a DID sufferer's daily life, there are some normal experiences, but consider these profound differences:

- how the person expresses himself with people
- what he remembers
- who he remembers
- his sense of relationship with people, even his own family
- how he experiences time
- how he sees things around him
- how he perceives money
- his sense of right and wrong

DID is the most extreme of all the dissociative conditions. It begins in childhood as the way a tiny mind adapts to overwhelming stress. It is what a vulnerable, young, trance-prone human being does to protect himself inside.

Dissociative fugue. A person with dissociative fugue (also known as a psychogenic fugue) is fleeing something overwhelming in his life, but that dissociative escape may happen only once as opposed to over and over again. The person will go into a different state of mind, and as part of that journey, will actually physically go someplace else. The person will remain there for a certain period of time—it could be hours or it could be days, months, or year—and do bizarre things; at least they seem bizarre relative to what went before. Most fugues don't involve the formation of a new identity, although they may involve the use of a different name. When different identities do emerge, they are usually characterized by more gregarious and uninhibited traits than those of the core person. During the fugue state, the person won't know where he is or what he's doing. Usually, the state will spontaneously resolve and, when it does, the person may well find himself in a strange place with all of the memories of his regular life intact, but no recollection of what happened in the fugue state. He may even end up in a different city and have no idea how he got there, but he'll know where he came from.

According to the DSM, the prevalence rate for this condition is .02 percent in the general population, so in the United States, that would translate to about 60,000 people. You'll find fugue as part of the plot in a few movies, but some of the most prominent cases raise serious doubts about their credibility (such as novelist Agatha Christie's mysterious disappearance in 1926 just after her husband's affair fueled gossip throughout England).[7] Because fugue commonly resolves in a spontaneous recovery, it's possible we don't have more cases to discuss because many of the people who've experienced it don't end up in therapy or emergency rooms.

Dissociative amnesia. In this condition (also known as psychogenic amnesia), which is much more common than the previous two, the person lacks the ability to recall important personal information. It's usually associated with a repeated unpleasant experience in childhood rather than a single event, although it can have roots in a single event, as in the case of Dan. Dan survived a plane crash in which a friend was killed and does not recall events immediately before the crash or anything about the crash. This is not a case of simple amnesia due to brain trauma that destroyed the memory trace. The memories still exist; they are just buried.

It's important here to differentiate between Dan's amnesia and the amnesia about an entire childhood that a victim of abuse might suffer. If a person has amnesia for an event, but no impairment in his social life, no impairment in his occupational or academic functioning, and no internal distress, then he has amnesia for an event, but not a disorder. There's nothing wrong with it. On the other hand, a person who has no memory of her childhood before a certain age and who feels as though a piece of her life is missing, does have a dissociative disorder—namely dissociative amnesia.

Often, the impetus for dissociative amnesia might be something like an abusive parent saying over and over again, "you're a bad child" or "you're just like your father." The child will grow up to have a generalized difficulty remembering his childhood. I have had a number of people in therapy tell me their memory of childhood is a blank before a particular age like nine or ten. What it usually means in terms of the defensive operations of the child is that he either didn't record or can't recall whole blocks of time for the sake of "forgetting" overwhelmingly painful memories.

From a neuroscience perspective, amnesia in the absence of brain damage can be partially explained in biochemical terms. Stress causes a chemical reaction that affects regions of the brain responsible for memory. With repeated overwhelming stress, neurotransmitters and stress hormones are released in the brain in such excess quantity that they can adversely affect portions of the brain responsible for emotional memories as well as other kinds of memory.

There is another intriguing angle in the amnesia discussion, as there is with many phenomena related to the mind. *False memory syndrome* would allow a person to fill in the blanks of childhood memories with bits and pieces of stories she heard. For example, an adult asserts she has a memory of something that happened when she was a toddler. It's possible the memory is factual. It's also possible that she heard a story from her grandmother and that story became transformed into an autobiographical memory. A variation of this for the person affected by dissociative amnesia involves filling spaces in childhood memories with details that "ought to be there," like pleasant memories of Christmas mornings.

This became a point of contention in the psychoanalytical community during Sigmund Freud's career, and it was instigated by Freud himself. Early in his career, Freud worked on the assumption that the memories that his patients were recalling, whether in the hypnotic state or the regular state of consciousness, were literal memories of being sexually traumatized as children. But then he began to espouse the notion that, at least in some cases, they weren't memories of what actually occurred. Rather, they represented fantasies that the child had at the time of sexual activities with the parent. Then later, they would remember them as though the incidents really occurred. That obfuscated the whole area of recalled memory and contributed to shaping the concept of false memory syndrome. The field of forensic psychiatric testimony in these cases of alleged sexual abuse took a hard hit. Defense teams began to lean heavily on the concept of false memory to defend their clients. Mental health professionals have to be assiduously careful about how we question patients—particularly children—on the subject of childhood sexual abuse because of how suggestible people can be. A person in middle childhood is in an especially suggestible phase of life; the trance capacity is at its peak. Asking a leading question like, "What did your daddy do to you?" undermines the believability of the response. From the perspective of someone who understands suggestibility and the differential vulnerability of different minds to be influenced about how they remember things, I discourage this kind of leading question in any context, forensic or otherwise.

What we've come to learn is that each act of remembering is different from the previous act of remembering. When you remember a Thanksgiving dinner five years ago right now, you will remember it differently from when you remembered it three years ago. In other words, remembering is an act of the present. A memory will be at least nominally distorted by the context in which you remember it. Suppose I said to you, "Thanksgiving dinners often seem to work out as happy events no matter what goes wrong." Given the context of my saying that to you, you might conclude, "Come to think of it, I tried a new stuffing recipe and it turned out so dry, I was really embarrassed. But we just put a lot of gravy on it and laughed it off." Maybe the stuffing was a tiny bit dry, but in your new context of remembering, you recall it as having the appearance of shredded cardboard. As a corollary, a fact well known by interrogators is that the longer a person is removed from the incident about which he's being questioned, the more likely memory pollution will affect the story. Humans have a natural tendency to try to make sense of what they have observed or even dreamed and will insert details on an as-needed basis to do that. In the course of revising the memory or dream, they might also omit painful elements without meaning to do so.

On November 19, 1941, the Australian warship *Sydney* engaged in battle with a German ship called the *Kormoran* and both sank. The only survivors were about three hundred German sailors, who eventually were rescued and captured by the Australian military. The Australians tried diligently to get the Germans to give them the location where the ships went down, but so many conflicting reports emerged that the Australians could only conclude they heard lie after lie. The roughly seventy responses they'd collected placed the battle in locations that varied by hundreds of miles in some cases. It took more than five decades for those reports of the German sailors to make sense. Two cognitive psychologists, Kim Kirsner and John Dunn, finally put the pieces together and recognized the correlation between the stories the Germans provided and data that resulted from their experiments in the vagaries of memory. The Germans were not lying. The variances and shifts in their story corresponded to normal distortions in their recall. The work of Kirsner and Dunn led a professional shipwreck hunter to find the wrecks of the *Sydney* and the *Kormoran* in 2008.

The story is one more illustration of how current scientific knowledge can "correct" assumptions about what's going on in the human mind. Disorder? Normal adaption? Deceit? We have to keep asking the questions in light of what we know, keeping in mind that there's a lot we still don't know.

Depersonalization disorder.   In this case, the person gets a feeling of being detached from his or her own mental processes or body. Depersonalization experiences are rather common, so the disorder refers to the fact that they are repeated or persistent. The clinical name for them when they occur as you're drifting off to sleep is *hypnagogic hallucinations.* When they occur as you're just waking up, they're called *hypnopompic hallucinations.* Again, most of these sleep-related experiences are harmless, although they may be unsettling.

Depersonalization can take a number of different forms. One of them is a curious state we call the Isakower phenomenon,[8] named after the psychoanalyst Otto Isakower who described it in a 1936 article on mental disorders associated with falling asleep. He described an experience that patients told him about in which their sense of personal boundary repeatedly expanded and contracted in a very unsettling manner. I witnessed this in Sally, a patient with chronic complex post-traumatic stress disorder; ultimately, she stopped experiencing it as she grew healthier. She admitted to me reluctantly, because she didn't want me to think she was psychotic, that during sessions she experienced feeling herself moving toward and away from me. It wasn't a simple matter of perceiving a strong connection to me at one moment and a sense of distance at another. In her mind, she believed she was physically moving closer or farther away.

Technically, this is not a hallucination, an illusion, or a delusion. Instead, it is a form of depersonalization, or derealization, that is, a phenomenon dissociative in nature and not hallucinatory in the strictest sense of the word. In the state of derealization, a person perceives circumstances as a dream or in a fog.

Isakower phenomenon is somewhat akin to another type of depersonalization wherein the person experiences himself outside his body looking down. Again, if this happens repeatedly, it signals a disorder, but there are variations of it we don't associate with mental illness. Sometimes people going under anesthesia will experience the sensation of looking down on their bodies, and certain street drugs will trigger the same kind of sensation. Some near-death experiences also entail this out-of-body sensation.

It's important to explore a tangential subject here so that we don't get stuck in looking at these phenomena in two-dimensional terms. There are obviously people who think of a near-death experience in terms of spiritual transcendence rather than a psychiatric phenomenon. There is no need to think of it in either/or terms. That's a big mistake that the "biological reductionists" make. They think that if there is a brain-basis for an experience, then it can't be spiritual in nature. (A reductionist equivalent is saying that Michael Jordan wasn't a great basketball player—he just had muscles that worked well.) To say that a spiritual experience is spurious because you can show something changing in the brain doesn't make sense. There is no logical inconsistency between understanding such phenomena at the level of brain and talking about them at the level of spirit.

The great comedian Steve Martin describes a kind of depersonalization in his book *Born Standing Up* when he talks about himself on stage: "My most persistent memory of stand-up is of my mouth being in the present and my mind being in the future."[9] While his mouth and body delivered the lines, his mind focused on what to say next. He describes being displaced in time and space.

Let's take the notion of that displacement to a pathological extreme. Most people have experienced *déjà vu* and some have experienced *jamais vu*, both of which are kinds of depersonalization/derealization experiences, but just imagine experiencing that spatially and temporally disjointed world on a frequent basis.

In déjà vu, you're in a place or a situation where you know you've never been before; yet there is an intense familiarity to it and even a sense that you can predict what happens next. In jamais vu, you're at a place where you've been many times, but you feel you've never been there before.

Both are depersonalization experiences in the sense that the person experiences a powerful sense of either connection to an unknown location and/or situation, or a distance from a location and/or situation that should seem quite familiar.

An occasional accompaniment of déjà vu is that you have the sense that you can predict what will happen next. The paradox is that you can and you can't. You may be right or you may be wrong about that prediction. Maybe on later recollection you remember that you are right about what happens next all the time, but consider this: For normal people, that feeling of déjà vu leaves. Is it a "wrong" prediction that breaks the spell? Is it a "right" prediction that breaks the spell? You really don't know.

Put yourself in this situation. You are in a restaurant within sight of the women's restroom. You experience déjà vu and conclude that the restroom door is about to open—in fact, you even say it out loud: "That door's going to open." Let's take a look at how the Apollonian and the Dionysian person might handle such a "prediction." The empirical way of knowing, which would be the Apollonian approach, is concluding that it would be logical that the bathroom door would open if there are people periodically going in and out. The Dionysian person would assign the prediction to an intuitive perception. Who's to say which is "right"?

DISORDER AND/OR GENIUS?

The Amazing Kreskin (yes, that's his legal name) asserted that his ability to hypnotize an audience and "predict" events had their roots in SEP (scientifically explained phenomena) and not ESP (extrasensory perception). The caveat he would add is that we may not be able to explain the occurrence scientifically at the moment, but we would someday. When I mentioned this to Maryann, it reminded her of something a nun said in her junior-year religion class in high school: The miracles of Jesus will be explained by science someday. The fact that they couldn't be explained by science at the time they occurred makes them miracles.

How do you explain the fact that I can push a couple of buttons on my cell phone and get the score of the Phillies' game going on? Highly organized energy is all around us and our gadgets receive it and deliver it to us so we can access information. We have simply figured out how to make that happen. It makes sense to us with our current technological awareness that, in this huge electromagnetic spectrum all around us, information is available to us if we have the right receivers.

One of the features of trance-prone people is that they are able to accept knowledge in ways other than the five basic senses. The Apollonian person gathers information through the five basic senses, otherwise it's not real. The Dionysian person doesn't care if the information comes from a source other than the five senses; gut feeling has relevance and perhaps even priority in terms of a source of knowledge. This is how Albert Einstein could come up with a theory to which the empirical data of the time could not lead him, yet ultimately was embraced as a truth by the scientific community.

Can we conclude, therefore, that people like The Amazing Kreskin and Albert Einstein are highly trance-prone people? I would say, "Yes." They aren't shackled by a system of knowing governed only by the five senses, or by what is currently "known."

Saroj Parida responds to the world like Kreskin and Einstein. He earned the nickname "the infant whisperer"[10] long before his DID diagnosis, by seemingly using more than his five senses to treat seriously ill newborns. In his practice as a neonatologist, he seemed to have conversations with infants and sense what was wrong with them. Certainly his track record of saving tiny lives suggested that he had a rare sensitivity to their condition. On one occasion, he worked on an infant for forty-five minutes after the rest of his medical team concluded the baby had died. Saroj sensed life—and he was right. He was able to revive the infant who went on to health and normalcy.

Saroj learns in a very Dionysian way. I would describe it as more automatic than methodical. When he was twelve, his family moved from a small mining town to a larger city and he was enrolled in a school of English-speaking children; he spoke no English. Within six months, his math teacher invited him to conduct classes! He entered a top medical school at the age of fifteen—another phenomenal illustration of his ability to absorb information. His mind has a scarcely explainable way of accumulating knowledge, and I am sure it is not done in a conventional, empirical fashion. It's an intuitive and creative way of incorporating new information into the fabric of his mind. All of that gives him a distinct advantage when it comes to analyzing and addressing situations such as those involving critically ill infants.

He has many recollections of watching himself deliver lectures, very much like the depersonalization experiences described by Asia expert Robert Oxnam during some of his presentations. Oxnam details his life with DID and subsequent integration in *The Fractured Mind*. Saroj would think, "Holy smokes! Look at that guy—he's good!" And then, like Oxnam, he might give such a highly creative answer to a question from the audience that he would surprise himself, truly wondering how he could have concocted such a dazzling response.

Theoretical physicists say there are probably as many as fourteen dimensions. We are only operating in three at the moment. What's going on in the rest of them? We should all accept that not knowing the answer provides some validation to the idea that phenomena such as depersonalization and déjà vu are other than just imaginings of crazy people.

What Causes the Need to Dissociate?

$\mathcal{U}$p to this point, I have continued to weave the thread of choice throughout the discussions of dissociation because those who choose to utilize their trance capacity are, in fact, dissociating. They have some measure of control over whether or not the daydream or hypnosis occurs. As we take the journey toward the other side of the mirror, I will talk more and more about the need to dissociate, rather than the choice.

THOUGHTS, FEELINGS, AND PHYSIOLOGY

In the most generic sense, dissociation can be not only a dissociation from the various senses of the body, but also a dissociation from the emotional brain. (Some clinicians refer to those deeper regions of the brain that seem to be involved in emotion as the "limbic system," and I notice that this term is working its way into lay conversation. Although anatomically the idea of a distinctive region of the brain where emotion is located is overly simplistic, we will see later that there is definitely some usefulness in thinking of it that way.) First, let's look at this in terms of choice and need.

A person can choose to dissociate to mitigate pain, as Maryann did with a post-hypnotic suggestion during a surgical procedure. A person can also choose to dissociate emotionally by daydreaming about heading for the beach while sitting in a dreary office cubicle. A person can also have the need to dissociate to mitigate pain, as is often the case in wartime when a wounded soldier has no experience of pain until the mission is over and the requirement to stay mission-focused abates. Or in the case of a sexually abused child, the need to dissociate from the emotional brain blocks devastating memories.

Now look at these dissociations in physiological terms. Pain is experienced at the level of the cortex of the brain, the outermost layer of the brain where we believe consciousness is mediated. The sensory relay station called the thalamus is a deep brain structure that transfers signals from the spinal cord to the cortex. If something interrupts those signals at the thalamic level, the pain experience will be modified or even totally inaccessible to consciousness. One interesting area of pain research asks the question, "What sort of circuitry is involved in attenuating the signals going from the thalamus to the cortex?" One thing we do know: when people are depressed, their experience of pain is amplified. That hints at the likelihood that depression inhibits the circuits that would otherwise calm the pain signals.[1]

The story of Phineas Gage dramatically illustrates a physiological cause for dissociation from the emotional brain. Gage was a Gandy dancer, a man who helped build the railroad in the mid-1800s. A crew foreman with an impeccable reputation, he exhibited very caring behavior with his men. While working on a railroad in Vermont, his crew had responsibility for blasting through rock to prepare the roadbed. The process involved drilling a hole, putting the explosive in, bringing the primer cord out, and then filling the hole with sand and tamping it down so that when the charge went off, it didn't all blow up through the hole but instead sideways, rupturing the rock. One day, the crew set the charge and Phineas apparently wasn't quite paying attention and thought the hole was already filled with sand, went to tamp it, and inadvertently set off the charge. That blew the tamping rod through his cheek and out the top of his brain. The men around him later recalled that he seemed not to even have lost consciousness, and were astounded that, except for some blood loss, he seemed all right!

He had a somewhat challenging recovery, but doctors who examined him as he regained his physical strength determined that he apparently hadn't lost any cognitive ability. But, sadly, subsequently he began to behave in a bizarre fashion, displaying extremely antisocial behavior. Although accounts vary regarding the degree of Gage's misbehavior, he reportedly became sexually promiscuous and hostile—in other words, the two classic basic instincts, sexual and aggressive, seemed to be totally *disinhibited*. We now call that *frontal release behavior*, meaning that the frontal cortex of the brain that mediates conscience and executive functions, such as knowing how to behave, was totally severed from the limbic—that is, the emotional—brain. Phineas Gage's limbic brain was apparently destroyed, but his cognitive brain survived intact.

This is a classic case used to illustrate what happens when thought becomes dissociated from feeling. The emotional brain mediates social behavior; human beings need it if they want to live in community with other human beings. Neurologist António Damásio's work related to Gage may have earned him some criticism, but his core point has great value: We can't separate thought from feeling.[2] When thought gets dissociated from feeling, it becomes useless, if not dangerous.

A common situation in which a person becomes disinhibited involves abuse of alcohol and/or drugs. This chemical disinhibition differs from Gage's traumatic disinhibition in both cause and duration. One would hope that, when the scotch wears off, the twenty-something (or sixty-something, not to pick on twenty-somethings) who runs down Main Street naked will realize that the scotch did some temporary damage to his sense of social propriety. With Gage, there was no waking up such a realization. Certain forms of dementia, referred to a *frontotemporal dementia*, involve the experience of disinhibition as well. In those cases, the frontal lobes are disintegrating. People suffering from this may eat uncontrollably or become sexually promiscuous, among other things. If you've ever known someone who smoked marijuana and ate six bags of Oreos, you've seen a version of frontal disinhibition.

As is the case in some of the disorders briefly described in chapter 2, substance abuse can cause hallucinations as well as disinhibition. The people having them aren't necessarily disconnected from their emotional center as was Gage, but they experience a distortion of emotions as part of their altered sensory experience of reality. The common denominator between drug-induced and non-drug-induced hallucinations is neurotransmission. A person can slip into a dissociated state with exogenously administered drugs that affect the central nervous system. The most common adaptive examples of that are anesthetics. They are operating on nerve circuits that may be the same nerve circuits that get disabled temporarily in a dissociative experience. We're "asleep" when we miss an exit sign on the highway because we're daydreaming and we're "asleep" under anesthesia. In one case, the circuitry is being activated artificially, and in the case of dissociated trance, it happens naturally.

The *catecholamine hypothesis* of psychosis, in which people hallucinate, holds that there is too much activity of a brain chemical messenger called *dopamine* at certain parts of the brain. The so-called antipsychotic medicines block dopamine transmission. In contrast, someone who has hallucinations in a dissociated state is not likely to respond to that kind of chemical solution—they might, but it's not likely. So people with a functional psychosis such as schizophrenia or bipolar mania may also experience hallucinations, but again, they are believed to be linked to a structural or intrinsic biochemical malfunction in the brain, unlike the individual who hallucinates in the midst of dissociative experiences.

ROOTS OF THE NEED TO DISSOCIATE

People with a high trance capacity seem to use dissociation as a default coping mechanism in the face of trauma. There are other neurobiological factors that simply make some people more likely to dissociate than others.

Trauma also need not be defined in terms of abuse, neglect, or horrible accident. For some, trauma may be the very unique kind of stress of being a child prodigy. Of course for some, such as neonatologist Saroj Parida, who entered a highly ranked and demanding medical school at the age of fifteen, the factors of abuse and prodigy intertwined to render dissociation an ever-more frequently dysfunctional event in his life.

Ultimately, trauma is a subjective experience. Two people having the same negative event, or series of events, in their lives can have very different responses. One might end up affected for life and the other might put it behind her and move on.

Before a student skydiver makes her first jump—not a skydive while attached to a tandem pilot, but an independent skydive accompanied by two instructors—she has about six hours of training. The combination of classroom study and practical training prepares the student for myriad "what ifs." Even though that student will be flanked by two professional skydiving instructors, without the mental and physical preparation for various contingencies, she's taking an unnecessary risk.

During that first skydive, paradoxical feelings put many students into sensory overload. They are flying, yet falling; have unprecedented awareness of surroundings, yet see nothing but white space; are shocked by the noise and stunned by the silence. Let's say the skydive involved a gear malfunction for one of the instructors. The student sees the instructor calmly handle it and thinks, "That's what all the training is about." The rest of the jump goes well and the student's dominant memories are flying like a bird with a serene sensation of moving toward the horizon over green pastures. The skydive represents a thoroughly happy experience on which she can build to make more skydives; with each one she gains the ability to address more "what ifs."

In contrast, let's say another skydiver sees the instructor handle the malfunction calmly, but flashes to the question, "What if that were me?" and concludes, "I wouldn't know what to do!" She is distracted and her mind wanders from the skydive for a split second as her mind embraces the thought "I could die!" The fact that her mind wandered, and she's aware it, compounds the sensory overload. She suddenly can't wait for the jump to end so she can feel safe again.

Why does the exact same experience result in reassurance for one person—an actual increase in her sense of safety—and trauma for another person, who experiences a complete loss of feeling safe? As a corollary, in the first case, the student will likely daydream about more flying and more fun, and as a result, likely keep improving in the sport. But the second student will have nightmares (or "daymares") long after the jump ends. One experience of mind wandering is healthy and confidence building, and the other, corrosive to the person's sense of confidence.

The answer to "why" could be complex, or potentially quite simple. Perhaps the first student skydiver's childhood involved instances in which an authority figure, perhaps a parent, made some obvious good choices when confronted with difficulty and everything turned out fine. Perhaps the second skydiver had the opposite kind of experience; she remembers things going wrong in the face of adversity. Whatever the reason, her threshold for trauma in this situation is quite different.

All of the dissociative disorders arise from a person's need to cope with adversity and establish a sense that "everything's okay." In the example above, the first student skydiver felt safe in the sky, but the second one felt her safety threatened and would do everything possible to avoid the feeling again.

Abraham Maslow's hierarchy of needs adds another dimension of understanding to the contrasting responses. In the hierarchy, food and shelter are the basic needs, but right above that are safety and security. Maslow postulated that a person could not go to the next level of human connection until the baser needs were met—that it simply was not possible for a person to meet higher needs like relationship and self-esteem in any meaningful way until he perceived that the basic needs were met. Maslow developed his theory after studying healthy people free of mental illness, because he determined that their responses would yield more reliable results. So the point I'd make is that the need to feel safe is a normal impulse that drives all of us to some degree.[3]

Imagine you have a sense of being protected, and suddenly it's gone. Put yourself in the jumpsuit of student skydiver number two. You land safely, breathe a sigh of relief, take off your gear, and have a beer. Life has regained the order you prefer and now you feel like a party. But wait, like Bill Murray in the movie *Groundhog Day*, the entire event begins to repeat itself. Someone keeps forcing you back into the plane and shoving you out the door.

In a way, that is the kind of surreal torture experienced by children repeatedly subjected to sexual abuse. The story of Saroj Parida's early life illustrates why Saroj, a highly trance-prone individual, had the need to dissociate in order to cope with the constant threat and persistent reality of sexual violation.

As a baby, Saroj loved the smell of food and he crawled off a piece of furniture in the family's courtyard in an effort to reach the dining table. His family lived in a former British mining town in rural India, and reminders of mines were everywhere. When he fell, a pointed piece of gravel embedded itself near his eye. He bled profusely, soaking one side of his mother's sari with blood. There was only one doctor in town and he was away at the time, so his parents went with the usual "plan B" in such instances—the pharmacist, who in India was known as a "compounder." He took a needle and thread used for stitching clothes and sewed the wound shut.

Now more than 50 years old, Saroj still bears a indentation very near his eye from the incident. A cut or a few stitches on a small child will be almost unnoticeable on the adult, but this wound was so deep and stitches so coarse that the scar remains quite visible.

When Saroj was five years old, the sexual abuse began. In India, it's common to have a servant, or caretaker; even households without much wealth will have someone living in the household whose job is to do tasks around the house and perhaps watch the children. Saroj's parents hired a twelve-year-old servant when Saroj was just an infant. Young adolescents commonly work in India. They took him in, and treated him like another son. When Saroj was five years old, the young man began to talk about his girlfriends and bring pictures of naked women into the house. As he tucked Saroj into bed, he began to fondle him.

Knowing the background makes it clear why Saroj never told his parents. British mine owners ruled the town and owned palatial estates where they had parties. Sometimes Saroj's parents would be invited to the festivities. This is one of the many types of occasions that drew Saroj's parents away from home in the evening. His parents were very young and understandably wanted to have fun; his mother was still in her late teens when she had Saroj's older brother, and in her early twenties when she had Saroj. The older brother had gone to live with grandparents when he was little, and then went to boarding school after that.

When his parents would leave for an evening, Saroj was just a little boy in need of the stability and security that all children need. His brother was gone; he would worry that his parents might not come back, too. His vivid imagination would concoct terrible outcomes; he would shake. The young man in charge of him would try to soothe him. At first, he just rubbed his leg. Eventually, his "soothing" involved the genitals. "Don't tell anyone. This is our secret," he insisted.

Personalities, or alters, emerged as a result of young Saroj trying to cope with this repeated trauma. The alters had a defensive function, so they subserved the negative emotions stirred up by the trauma. The alters were repositories of negative emotion so that his core personality could experience some sense of normalcy and happiness. Imagine, if you will, even the short list of overpowering emotions that the young Saroj had to sequester into dissociated nooks and crannies of his mind in order to survive emotionally: fright, rage, confusion, a mind-crushing admixture of sexual arousal, guilt and shame, helplessness—and that is not nearly a complete list.

DISSOCIATIVE BAND THEORY

During his incarceration, Saroj Parida has had lots of time to consider the mental state that brought him there. In correspondence and conversation with me and Maryann, he talked a great deal about paradoxes in his life, the central one of which was his yin-yang relationship with dissociation. He values it for what he believes it allowed him to accomplish, and despises it for corrupting his life.

Out of this came his *dissociative band theory*. To explain it, I ask that you imagine yourself sitting at a typical picnic table, the top composed of three slats of wood parallel to each other and "invisibly" bound together. The slat in the middle represents the everyday, normal band of dissociation involving such routine mind wandering as daydreaming. At the top border of that band is the Dionysian state of mind; at the bottom, the Apollonian.

Move to the slat, or band, just "above" the central one—that is, farther away from you. This is the realm into which the extreme Dionysian individual can spontaneously or at times intentionally traverse (as in deep meditation or hypnotic trance). This is where Einstein created new theories in a trance state, where Angelina Jolie embodies characters in a screenplay, where Saroj Parida would emerge into a zone that allowed him save critically ill babies by "hearing" their "whisper."

Move to the slat, or band, just below the central one. This is the realm of the extreme Apollonian individual. This is where other physicists utilize reason to accommodate existing physical theory to Einstein's new discovery, where producers give Jolie the environment to act, where medical staff supported Saroj with state-of-the-art technology in neonatal intensive care units.

Now watch the long sides of the top of the picnic table bending downward and then approximating a fourth slat to form a new, cylindrical shape. What is that additional slat that joins the Dionysian in-the-zone slat and the Apollonian flow-of-logic-and-order slat? It represents that realm of extreme dissociation that arises out of a desperate need to make sense of the world. It is that extreme Dionysian mind damaged by the chaos of trauma and desperately trying to achieve artificially the sense of mental order, logical sequence, and relatedness that the Apollonian mind enjoys naturally.

It is this band of dissociation where Becky Young-Losee went when she was a child. The abuse began when she was in kindergarten and continued until she was eight years old, when her mother divorced the father who assaulted her. Fortunately, Becky had a best friend named "Berberlishes" who helped her put the hurt in a place where it couldn't be felt and assured her that someone would be by her side to make sense of the world. Unfortunately, for Becky that someone was unavailable in her external world and existed only in her mind in the "person" (alter) of Berberlishes.

This is also where Saroj's alters emerged, with each one assuming responsibility for an emotion or action that Saroj couldn't fit into his conscious world—anger over the abuse he endured, childlike needs for unconditional nurturing, and so on.

In fact, this matter of opposites being attracted to and finding each other seems to exist throughout nature, from magnets to human relationships. Consider politicians on the extremes of conservatism and liberalism. If the Republican candidate is too conservative, or the Democratic candidate too liberal, each has little chance of winning an election. Each must embrace enough of the good essence of the opposite philosophy so that the voter can imagine the person as realistic and trustworthy, rather than narrow-mindedly radical. Similarly, advocates for elimination of all prejudicial treatment begin with "live and let live." Choose whatever partner you want, practice any religion you want, enjoy whatever lifestyle suits you. Their counterparts on the other end discriminate because, to them, it seems logical and appropriate that choosing whatever partner, practicing any religion, or enjoying any lifestyle will engender societal chaos. In order to get the other side to agree to a more "live and let live" approach, the no-prejudice side establishes rules about how people must treat each other and what must be legally allowed. Ironically, by their very nature, those rules tend to establish prejudice because they codify practices of behavior that do not allow everyone to choose and act as he or she sees fit.

So in light of this, we can understand the tendency of the highly trance-prone person to dissociate under extraordinary stress as an effort to seek an Apollonian solution. In fact, we can understand dissociative identity disorder as an effort to bring order out of chaos by way of an organized group of alters, each responsible for "reasonably" managing a particular emotional need otherwise too overwhelming for the core person. This in turn renders the person able to feel "Apollonian enough" in routine everyday life.

CAN THE NEED DISAPPEAR?

As a step toward putting the severity of each of the dissociative disorders into perspective, consider two people with observable problems in terms of the three axes of symptoms, personality, and functioning.

Just looking at symptoms, two people might have the same degree of major depression with physiological features; for example, sleep disturbance, diminished appetite, and low energy level. But one of them is endowed with all kinds of mental strengths: good intellectual strength, stable temperament, great relationship capacity, good ability for affective expression, and just as significant as those internal characteristics, good social supports. The other one might have just the opposite: marginal intelligence, poor capacity for relatedness, poor ability for emotional expression, and social isolation. Even though they have the same degree of symptomatic severity by DSM diagnosis, one will likely do a lot better than the other one before, during, and after therapy. Similarly, in the case of dissociative disorders, envision them as just part of the overall picture of the person. Depending upon what the rest of the person's mental health picture is like, the prognosis might be better than that for another person even though the symptom severity for both might be the same. Carrying that argument even further, someone with an episode of psychogenic fugue might be in a lot more trouble than a person with DID, even though the latter is otherwise a more extreme dissociative disorder.

It seems there are two factors that determine the severity and persistence of a dissociative disorder. One is the overall mental health of the patient, as we have noted above and in the description of my broadened diagnostic approach. The other, as we will see in detail later, is treatment. If dissociation is essentially an effort of the mind to cope with psychological stress, then it stands to reason that one could learn more effective coping strategies. And that, in a nutshell, is the ultimate aim of therapy for dissociative disorders. Then the person of great psychological resilience who dissociates under enormous psychological stress is relatively unlikely to ever dissociate again unless another extraordinarily traumatic event occurs, and the person with an outright dissociative disorder is less likely to suffer further episodes of problematic dissociation if the disorder is properly and thoroughly addressed in therapy.

· 4 ·

Eccentric versus Sick:
Spotting the Difference

$\mathcal{T}$he former CEO of a major Silicon Valley company had a peculiar way of dealing with tension. According to those in his inner circle, he would occasionally curl up under his desk. Eccentric behavior? Yes, but does that suggest he has a mental illness?

Emma dressed Goth—black clothes, nails, lips, and hair—all the time. That did not stand in the way of a start-up company hiring her to do web design. The senior executives figured that customers would never see her, and so it didn't matter. They did not think through the fact that if the woman at the reception desk was out sick or on a break, then someone would have to rotate into the slot. Emma therefore covered the reception desk periodically in her eccentric all-Goth glory. Did that suggest she was in any way unstable?

I introduced Robert and Emily, the skydiving couple, in chapter 2. That incident of Robert swooping into a picnic with his parachute was not odd enough for Emily to suspect that he was anything other than a daredevil. That is, until a few months later, when Emily came home from a business trip to find Robert missing. The phone rang. "This is Steve from Skydive Deland. Your husband is running up and down an active runway. Can you come get him?" Deland, Florida, was at least a twelve-hour drive from their home in Washington, DC. Emily immediately headed for the airport and flew to Orlando, where Steve picked her up. When she arrived at Skydive Deland an hour later, Robert was asleep in his car. The next day, they had a strange drive back to DC, with Robert seeming chipper and asking, "What are you so worried about, babe?" Immediately upon their arrival at home, Emily went into the house and Robert snagged the car keys and disappeared again. This time, with the help of the police, Robert got an escort to the hospital where he spent the next month in the psychiatric unit.

Christa was born on Christmas Day to a family whose religious sect held that babies born on Christmas Day carried a curse. Members of her family wanted her dead, a sentiment so infused into her life that she could not escape a sense of worthlessness. Her mother's family and friends within the church community repeatedly reminded her parents that they should have gotten rid of Christa when she was born. "They told me this when I was little and they discussed it in front of me," she recalls. Friends in her mother's bridge group who shared her religious beliefs would not come to the house if they knew Christa was home. One day she was home sick and her mother's church friends came over for bridge. Her mother gave Christa strict orders to stay upstairs while they were there. But instead, she pulled out a cape that had been part of a Halloween costume and ran down the stairs and around the women, all the while making screeching sounds. Many people would dismiss Christa's antics as those of a feverish, unruly child. Christa's mother and her friends, however, assumed this affirmed their suspicion that Christa was cursed. Years later as an adult in therapy, she surmised that the event was, in fact, very likely an early emergence of her alter named Judge.

THE NATURE OF IMPAIRMENT

The Silicon Valley executive and Emma the Goth may have seemed eccentric to those around them, but their oddness is markedly different from that of Robert and Christa. Going back to the DSM's diagnostic criteria, we would have to conclude that the first two suffered no impairment as a result of engaging in this mildly odd activity. On the other hand, Robert and Christa were functionally impaired in terms of relationships and, as I discuss later in the chapter, in terms of career as well.

Synonyms for "impair" include ruin, mess up, damage. So in terms of mental illness, the nature of impairment is that some part, or maybe all parts, of a person's life are ruined, messed up, damaged.

Contrast the executive—whose career is still moving along well—and the Goth—whose talents helped her score big when the start-up went public—with the felon, Dr. Saroj Parida. He is both eccentric and has a dissociative disorder. Some of his unusual behaviors fell into that normal spectrum of a high performer who gets "into the zone" or "spaces out" or "acts weird." The people around him who made excuses for him had every reason to be confused and, in fact, to wonder if he was faking a mental illness when he later got caught perpetrating insurance fraud. How could a physician who saved one infant after another from death—sometimes almost miraculously—be mentally impaired?

If we see a person as "odd" or "eccentric" but without any obvious signs of impairment, we tend not to consider that oddity as possibly indicative of serious mental illness. When Saroj committed insurance fraud, fellow physicians were inclined to conclude that he was odd and a sociopath, rather than seeing his eccentricity as being symptomatic of pathology such as dissociative identity disorder.

Shortly after I started treating Saroj, I went to a party that included a number of area physicians who knew him. They didn't know I was his psychiatrist. He had just made the headlines with the fraud allegations, so the room was abuzz with judgments and speculations. Understandably, they were disdainful of the antisocial behavior that he had shown with the crimes. They bandied about terms like *malignant narcissism*, meaning he was a self-centered, self-absorbed individual with an entitled narcissistic personality disorder. It's a conclusion some drew about Saroj's state of mind based largely on the fact that his lecture style and social demeanor seemed arrogant and haughty. The less abrasive ones left off the word "malignant" and just described him as a genius who was full of himself.

Not one of them was inclined to reserve their immediate, critical judgment. These are really very good and very compassionate doctors—medical professionals trained to allow for all possible diagnostic explanations of their patients' behavior. Sadly, they gave no more considered thought about the condition of Saroj Parida's mental state than anyone else reading the local newspaper, who just concluded that he was a crook with a great education. Not one of them asked the question, "Gee, I wonder if he has a mental illness, so he might be impaired?"

The preeminent researcher in developmental trauma disorders, Bessel A. van der Kolk, talks about three categories of dissociation, which he calls primary, secondary, and tertiary.[1] His descriptions and sorting stand in complement to those in DSM-IV that I covered in chapter 2, but for purposes of gaining insight to both the "how" and "why" of a dissociating person's impairment, they serve us well. To make it simple, I'm going to call them Type 1, Type 2, and Type 3.

Type 1 dissociation involves a re-experiencing of the original trauma. The past affect associated with the original trauma resurfaces, triggered by some current circumstance, and the person will, in effect, emotionally identify the current circumstance with the original trauma. It's possible for a person to go into a kind of daydream state and relive the trauma as a flashback. But what van der Kolk focused on was the traumatic memory wherein the original emotion is attached to the current circumstance. Instead of seeming like a daydream, it has the jolt of present reality. This is exactly what Charlie, a young veteran of two tours of duty in Iraq, has been going through; his story also shows how the United States Army is helping him make changes to address the problem.

When Charlie first sought help for PTSD, the Army administered a test to determine his capacity for dissociation; he tested extremely high. He would relive traumas, even in safe, protected environments like at a family friend's house when he heard a balloon pop and dropped to the ground, his reflexes telling him it was gunfire. After Charlie went into the intensive outpatient program for trauma and recovery provided by the Army at Fort Carson, he began receiving support and training to "relive *and* overcome." During a recent skydive in which he was supposed to fly toward other jumpers with the intent of building an in-air formation, he had a flashback. Suddenly he was back in Iraq with an "explosively formed penetrator" (EFP) whizzing so close to his head that he could feel the heat. An EFP is a particularly heinous type of roadside bomb and it took out the truck he was in. The "overcome" part of this experience is that Charlie did separate his memory from the reality of the moment and regain enough control to make the conscious decision to fly away from the formation to make sure he didn't do anything to jeopardize the safety of others. In retrospect, he realizes that the adrenaline that was integral to the skydive acted like a trigger for this episode. He had a sense that something was going wrong while still in the aircraft before exiting for the skydive: "On the plane ride up, it started coming back in droplets and then became a water hose. Soon, I was drowning in my memories."

Brain imaging suggests that the person with Type 1 (primary) dissociation is not, in fact, reflecting on the trauma and still staying connected to the current reality—the person with a primary dissociation partially relives the original trauma, involving a perceptual distortion that disconnects him from the current reality. To quote the authors of a study called "Neurobiology of Dissociation," those primary dissociative responses "involve the emotional and phenomenologic reliving of traumatic memories as if they are occurring at the moment of recall."[2] They demonstrated this with imaging studies that clearly indicated certain types of activity in the amygdala, the region of the brain that processes emotion and stores those emotional memories. The important thing to note about Type 1 is that the emotional memories associated with the original trauma are resurrected by a contextual cue in the present. The researchers induced the effect through experimental external stimuli, but ordinary life events are generally what cause the trauma-affected person to experience the real trauma—all of its sound and fury—as though it's happening at the moment.

In contrast to Type 1 dissociation, Type 2 is characterized by the person becoming distanced from the traumatic experience rather than reliving it. The depersonalization that occurs gives the person a sense of relief, as though she is watching someone else experience pain; it's as though an anesthesiologist entered the room and gave the person a sedative.

In the article "Neurobiology of Dissociation," the authors also addressed brain activity occurring during Type 2, which DSM-IV calls *peritraumatic dissociation*. They reference a unique opportunity to study the differences in that activity between the two types by doing imaging studies on a married couple that had a shared trauma: a horrific multivehicle car accident in which they were trapped and witnessed a child in another car burn to death. The husband had a Type 1 response when the team exposed him to stimuli capturing the event, and the wife had a Type 2 response.[3] Whereas he felt real pain and anxiety, she described herself as feeling numb and "frozen." Using scans, the research team could see the correlations between response and activation or shut-down in different regions of the brain.

A phenomenon possibly related to Type 2 dissociation is called *alexithymia*. People affected by it have trouble identifying the emotion they're experiencing. Multiple websites provide a self-report measure called the Toronto Alexithymia Scale, which features statements requiring a response ranging from "strongly agree" on one end of the spectrum to "strongly disagree" on the other.[4] One example: "People sometimes get upset with me, and I can't imagine why." Many sites provide a score afterward. Whether a person is diagnosed with a dissociative mental illness or not, anyone experiencing a state of alexithymia is impaired. It may be a temporary problem, but it is nonetheless a problem that, at the moment, is damaging the person's ability to relate to others.

Type 3 is dissociative identity disorder. Alters emerge to protect and defend the host from the trauma. Both the literature on this as well as my own experience confirms that these alters often have names that describe emotional states or emotional requirements of the host. For example, Christa's main alters are Silent and Judge. Saroj has, among others, Baby, Sissy, Giver, and those with Indian names suggesting sun, anger, and evil woman.

An important point here is that alters share memory. Whether it's Saroj's Baby or Ravana, his ferocious protector named after the Hindu god of anger, the alter has memories of his initial traumas, his marriage, his medical practice, his fraud. Memories recorded in a dissociated state are therefore not necessarily dissociated from the host personality, or any other personality, although the host is typically often consciously amnestic for those memories. That feature of Type 3 dissociation helps to explain why Saroj wasn't aware of his criminal acts and could not tell the FBI where the money was.

Neural imaging suggests there is not a particular brain region for each alter, but rather there is a parallel distribution throughout the various regions of the brain, just as there is with the host personality. There are connections all over the brain that give the different personalities all the life of the host: sensory and motor cortex, executive functions of the brain and sensory and motor cortices, and so on. As the research progresses, I imagine we will be able to illustrate the difference between a DID brain and a non-DID brain during certain provocative measures.

The case of ten-year-old Joey offers an example of at least Types 1 and 2 dissociation, and perhaps even Type 3. At initial evaluation Joey had a history of loosening and pulling out his teeth. He would hand them to his mother with no visible sign of anger or pain. He would simply avulse the tooth and then, at some point a little later, present it to his mother with an emotional nonchalance that unnerved her. As the treatment progressed, we learned that these episodes invariably followed a stormy emotional upheaval between Joey and his mother, wherein he felt the threat of abandonment.

When Joey was five years old, his mother was incarcerated for physically abusing him. Although never confirmed by actual recollection by the boy or his mother, it appeared more than plausible that he was struck in the face and mouth, causing a painful loosening if not loss of one or more teeth. It would follow then that subsequently at some level he would associate his mother's anger at him with the memory: mommy hits me, then the police take mommy away from me. (Children so depend on their parents that they are terrified of losing them no matter how abusive they might be. Also keep in mind that children tend to believe their parents' aggression against them is deserved, no matter how violent. Finally, as you will see in upcoming discussions of cases, children have some affection for their parents alongside however much fear they may have.) Members of Joey's treatment team in the day hospital program observed that he would suddenly "freeze" and seem petrified whenever he felt incapable of performing some task. They could only imagine how he must have felt at home when mother was not pleased with him. Thus, it was safe to assume that Joey was experiencing the reemergence of a traumatic memory, causing the "here-and-now" to feel just like the "then-and-there" to him—Type 1 dissociation.

Then the Type 2 dissociation would occur. In a depersonalized way, Joey would calmly walk into his mother's bedroom and present her with a tooth. He would get tremendous relief thinking that all he had to do to repair his relationship with his mother is to give her a tooth so the police wouldn't come and take her away. Now you might ask, why would he persist in giving her his teeth if she showed such revulsion at his doing so? The answer is found in the all-important psychoanalytic concept of the *compromise formation*. That is, our behavior often serves to take care of opposing needs simultaneously, sort of like hitting the snooze button in the morning to satisfy both the wish for just a little more delicious sleep and the need to face the day. Thus, if Joey is at once unconsciously terrified of losing his mother again and furious with her for being a mean mother, unnerving her by this indifferent presentation of yet one more tooth would quite efficiently satisfy both opposing emotions. (Oh yes, the human mind *is* more complicated than a computer!)

For some time I suspected that Joey also manifested Type 3 dissociation—dissociative identity disorder. Sometimes, he appeared to be a happy-go-lucky child who played well with others and tried to be unusually helpful to our treatment team. Other times, he'd suddenly be the self-abusive child. Still other times, he would simply withdraw emotionally. While Joey ultimately did not appear to have DID, he certainly did have the traumatic history and neuropsychological makeup of a child who could dissociate into alters.

In thinking about the nature of impairment, just about anyone would also wonder, "Are these people putting me at risk? Is someone who has multiple personalities not only impaired, but also potentially putting my safety at risk in the workplace or in the community?"

Clinically, I question the potential of persons with true DID to commit violent crimes *in an alter state*. That is, it seems to me that by definition, persons with DID originally achieved fundamentally integrated personality development as children prior to the onset of fragmentation of specific intolerable emotions into alters under the stress of trauma. And again by definition the integrated child personality is one with a core of solid conscience. The sociopathic/psychopathic personality is one that either occurs from failure of that initial integration in early childhood development or from some physical brain damage later on, such as occurred with Phineas Gage. So while the person with DID is just as capable of violence as anyone else when under the influence of mind-altering drugs, intolerable provocation, or brain damage, the DID itself does not render him more likely to commit violent crimes. In fact, the argument must be made that the mind's very act of sequestering destructive emotions into alters is in the name of other-preservation as well as self-preservation. In Saroj's instance, I never once worried that he would act out violently against family or others. His worrisome destructive potential was only against himself, such that I persuaded him not to borrow a gun from a neighbor, and several times talked him down from suicidal urges while standing at the edge of a quarry.

Christa bought a gun with the intention of committing suicide. Both Saroj and Christa "chickened out" as a judging, berating alter reminded them when they didn't go through with the suicide. In the case of Cameron West, who earned his PhD in psychology after going through years of successful integration therapy for his own DID, one of his alters did harm him—repeatedly—by cutting. In the prologue of his book *First Person Plural*, West describes a depersonalization experience in which he's "watching" his alter named Switch slice his right arm with a knife.[5] Much later, after West had been in therapy a while, Switch drew a picture of himself with the bold words "Help Me" above the body with a bloody right arm and a knife in the left hand. He admitted that he didn't want to hurt Cameron; he just didn't want to be ignored.[6] Similarly, Becky Young-Losee once woke up with bruises on her face and thought, once again, she'd been victimized by her spouse. For a change, he hadn't been the abuser; she'd done it to herself. Becky also recalls instances eerily similar to those self-mutilation experiences described by Cameron West. She had the sense of looking down on herself from the ceiling while she beat and stabbed herself. In her case, the alter crying out for help was a middle-aged woman known only as The Mother, the long-suffering alter who tried to absorb all the pain.[7]

DISGUISING THE IMPAIRMENT

Even before a diagnosis of mental illness, Robert had some sense of his impairment as it pertained to work. He had great skills as a skydiver and parachute rigger, and had earned a certification as an Airframe and Powerplant Mechanic, so he was qualified to fix airplanes. But anything that required regularity in his performance he knew was "not for him." He designed his life to take odd jobs and live a nomadic life until he married Emily, who naturally expected that he would put his skills to use in a job.

On the strength of her income, they bought a small house, but she expected Robert to kick in something toward the mortgage and household expenses. Just as her pressure to perform reached the point where he knew an ultimatum was coming, he took action. Emily came home from work one day to find the wall between the kitchen and living room demolished and debris all over the floor. Robert cheerfully announced that he had begun renovations of their home and knew she would be delighted with the result—which should be done in a year or two. In effect, he successfully disguised his impairment by creating a "job" that allowed him maximum flexibility in terms of hours and commitment.

Christa had two disguises and perpetuated them with no conscious understanding that she was doing it. First, like Saroj Parida, her impairment was disguised by the company she kept:

> I always assumed other people had experiences analogous to mine. That the manifestation might not be the same, but that we had something in common in terms of deficits in memory or performance. For example, I've

had friends who couldn't figure out how to make a pot of coffee, but could write optimization algorithms for complex supply chains in their sleep. I would dismiss their "shortcomings" the same way they would dismiss mine: You're so smart that you don't even take notice of some of the ordinary stuff of life because it's too boring for you. So the impression I got from people was, "You have bigger things to think about. No wonder you can't remember where you parked your car."

Secondly, Christa passed off incidents of forgetfulness and odd behavior by attributing it to a scuba diving accident in which she got Type 2 decompression sickness, which affects the brain. She honestly thought that the accident had caused some of the eccentricities and "spacing out" that people around her, most notably her wife Zoey, had noticed.

Persons with various other conditions involving memory impairment automatically develop ways to disguise their symptoms. I recall during my residency interviewing an elderly man with Wernicke-Korsakoff syndrome, also known as alcoholic encephalopathy and caused by a thiamine deficiency. These folks typically have large gaps in their memory for recent events, and fill in the gaps by way of *confabulation*, namely the creation of a fictitious story. This man had wandered away from his home and was missing for two days. His effort to account for his whereabouts and activities during those two days was almost comical were it not sad. He told me that he was busy figuring out new routes for a touring riverboat on the nearby Susquehanna River. He became indignant when I expressed some mild surprise. But his style of confabulation was so unhesitating and smooth that I'm sure many who would meet him on the street would consider him to be nothing but a BS-er.

Sometimes the "disguise" of the impairment is self-inflicted by the impaired person. On at least one occasion Saroj was contacted by one of the health insurance companies he'd inappropriately billed for services. He merely refunded the money requested by the company without questioning himself about how he could have submitted the invoices in an incredibly chaotic fashion. (For example, he would submit invoices dated for services provided to babies before they were even born!) These billing practices belied his superior intellect, and we finally recognized in his treatment that they had been occurring in dissociated states of mind. Therefore, Saroj was unable to "learn" from his billing mistakes and perpetuated them, ultimately leading to the arrest for insurance fraud.

Paradoxically, DID itself is both the best and the worst disguise for functional impairment. It is the best in that the alters frequently make it possible for the host personality to be productive, and perhaps even witty and uniquely talented. For example, Robert Oxnam had studied guitar, but played badly; it was one of his alters who displayed a musical gift. The flip side is that the alters are not like characters in a play, with well-scripted lines that move the action forward in a planned way. They don't have a unified vision for how their behaviors should affect outcomes. They can also assume variants in body language and voice that make the host come across like a bad actor instead of a person who is mentally ill.

When Judge comes out, people who don't know that Christa dissociates just think that she's in a "rude mood." It's as though she is pretending to be a fourteen-year-old boy with a bad attitude. Many other therapists have documented similar experiences, with their patients' alters coming across as bad acting.

My experience with the physicality of Saroj's alters was both similar and different. The similarity was in the voices, one of which seemed like a grown man pretending to a young, female child, and another a sophisticated man having the vocal expressions of a barnyard animal. The former involved a halting, babyish speech so the shift couldn't be missed. During the height of his legal and media turmoil, Saroj as Sissy (a characteristic Saroj sometimes assigned himself to describe the way he handled confrontation) called Maryann and left messages on her voice mail. She saved them because they provide excellent examples of the vocal change when Sissy emerged. He spoke in a soft voice, sometimes turning a sentence into a question, just as a child seeking approval would do.

In his first message on April 25, 2010, after he was convicted for insurance fraud but before he was sentenced, he left a message that began, "Hu, hu, hu, hullo" and then attempted to give a phone number. He tried completing the number a few times, just as a small child who is uncertain about a phone number might do. In the next message on June 18, a week after his sentencing hearing, Sissy seemed more like six or seven, rather than four or five years old: "I'm worried about Saroj . . . he's very upset. He trusts you. I don't know what I can do with him. He was fine and he's not so good now . . . sorry. Bye bye."

There was also a nonverbal alter even younger than Sissy that surfaced a couple of times for me. Saroj's Baby curled up on the front yard of the clinic one day after we had had a light snowfall. Having seen Saroj's car coming up the driveway from my office window, I went outside to see why he wasn't in the waiting room where I always greeted him at our appointment time. He was asleep in the snow in a fetal position with his fingers at his mouth. Later we would recognize Baby's function in protecting us both from Saroj's anger with me for being a few minutes late. Saroj was not comfortable displaying anger with me since I was his best hope for healing, but he was angry nonetheless. Baby took over, making it impossible to show his true negative feelings and ensuring that I would attend to him immediately since, after all, a caring person rushes to aid an endangered infant. Another alter spoke only the Indian dialect of Saroj's youth, so it was quite evident when he showed up.

Saroj had some other distinctive physical shifts related to his alters. One was diet. He is not a big man, certainly not overweight, but he has often eaten multiple meals of extremely different kinds depending on the cravings of his alters. His wife remembers one time when he took leftover McDonald's french fries and added them to a fine steak dinner. When he was at Otisville Correctional Camp, he also hid plates of food under his bed—a violation that elicited punishments until it was clear to the psychologist on staff that he did not do it maliciously or intentionally. He simply needed to feed one or more of his alters. He also wore reading glasses with various magnifications because his experience was that, at times, his near vision was far worse than at others.

EMBRACING IMPAIRMENT—PREDATORS ON THE MOVE

Affiliations of all kinds—religious, political, or anything cause-oriented—can engender exploitation of someone with a dissociative condition just as easily as they can reflect a healthy modus vivendi.

When Denise was fifteen, she refused to take a high school biology test on evolution because her religious beliefs were grounded in creationism. Denise was an intelligent and rational child. But for her the argument for evolution versus creationism was not grounded in reason, but instead in her belief system and the manner in which she adhered to it. Denise was what experts would describe as an *affiliative learner*. That is, she would take in the teachings of those with whom she felt a strong affiliation or sense of belonging, without needing to expose them to critical evaluation. In other words, she would accept or reject teachings "lock, stock and barrel." Therefore, for her there were no shades of gray in the matter of creationism, which was the view of the nature of the world within the religious community in which she was imbedded. Persons at the other extreme of learning style, the so-called *assimilative learners*, need to evaluate critically every jot and tittle of a concept before they can "believe" it. Either learning style has its advantages and disadvantages, and very bright and moral people exist at both ends of the spectrum. In reality, most lie in between these extremes and use both assimilation and affiliation to learn. We might wonder "what's the big deal" in the evolution-creation argument if we live somewhere in the middle, able to accept some tenets of both belief systems. But for Denise, her stand was necessitated by her strong affiliation with her religious community. She functioned effectively socially and academically and was an emotionally well-adjusted child.

Now, contrast the relatively normal way Denise handled her belief with that of people in cults. In *The True Believer*, Eric Hoffer described people who, because of their overwhelming need to feel affiliated with some cause, will forfeit their independent judgment. They will give themselves mindlessly to a cause and its charismatic leader. They would be highly trance-prone people, at least some of whom have moved over the line to "sick." The Heaven's Gate and Jonestown suicides provide two examples.[8]

We should not be naïve about the reality that some people—pastors, senators, doctors, generals, cult leaders, and even mothers and fathers—target people who manifest dissociative mental illness. With shocking ease, some of these people will lose their own personal agency in the engulfing, charismatic leadership of people like Jim Jones, founder of the People's Temple. If nothing else, Hoffer's insight points out the value of knowing where we fall on the spectrum of trance-prone (Dionysian) to non-trance-prone (Apollonian) people, since trance-prone people are more likely to "buy into the program." Again, please note that there's no necessarily "good" or "bad" in this discussion. Instead, knowing where we fall on the trance-prone spectrum alerts us to our own social and learning strengths as well as social and learning vulnerabilities. Otherwise stated, the person whose extreme Apollonian nature makes difficult any affiliation with even healthy, like-minded groups has the opposite dilemma, such as living a painfully isolated existence. Self-righteously apart is no more desirable than mindlessly belonging.

Hoffer's "true believers" are vulnerable to becoming convinced that an aberration has more value that what is "normal." Whether they are following a charismatic politician, corporate executive, or religious leader, they see some kind of eccentric behavior as positive and a radical belief system as desirable rather than recognizing them as what they are in psychiatric terms: manifestations of impairment.

In *Get People to Do What You Want*, interpersonal skills expert Gregory Hartley outlines the "mechanics of charisma" that a motivated individual—predatory or not—might use to convince people to embrace a lifestyle and/or belief system. In other words, he outlines the steps to get people to drink the Kool-Aid!

> When average people run into a highly charismatic person, what is it that they recall about the person? Everyone who has an encounter with a decidedly charismatic person recounts the story in very similar fashion, regardless of whether the encounter went well or ended in tragedy. Whether it was, "He made me feel as though I was the only person in the room," or "He made me feel as though he was divine," it is always about a *feeling* and not facts.[9]

Hartley points to a salient concept here in terms of the types of people who are the most likely victims of a charismatic predator: it's about feeling, not facts. If you quickly concluded that a Dionysian person might be more vulnerable, I would agree. And who are the people who cope with trauma by dissociating? The Dionysians.

Wikipedia describes charisma in both a secular and a religious way, with the former being "compelling attractiveness or charm that can inspire devotion in others."[10] Hartley asked the question, "How do you craft that?" He then takes a fascinating approach to understanding the power of charisma: Essentially, he proposes that charisma can be explained scientifically and therefore be "demystified." In a sense, he's taking an Apollonian perspective on a Dionysian experience. This sounds remarkably akin to George Joseph Kresge's (a.k.a. The Amazing Kreskin) insistence that his "magical" abilities are not ESP but a version of a scientifically explainable phenomenon he labeled "psychosonics."[11] (Interestingly, Kreskin warned about the increased vulnerability of persons to the charismatic leader when in crowds, as opposed to when alone. He cited the charisma of Hitler as a tragic case in point.)

The five steps for getting people to do what you want, as proposed by Hartley, are as follows:

1. Demonstrate value.
2. Recognize opportunity.
3. Grant an audience.
4. Create belonging.
5. Differentiate your target.[12]

The entire description of the steps comprises a chapter, but what I'm going to do is present the essence of the process with a focus on the reasons why a person who has a tendency to dissociate is particularly vulnerable to someone we might label charismatic.

Hartley suggests that the charismatic person projects some special and desirable feature that distinguishes him- or herself from the crowd. He offers the example of an FBI field agent who interviewed Saddam Hussein intensively over an extended period of time, posing as a high-level official in the service of the president of the United States. Hartley attributes Saddam's not discovering the ruse to the ego gratification he got out of believing that the U.S. president was so interested in him. Was Saddam a highly trance-prone individual—that is, Dionysian—who was so flattered by the agent's persistent interest in him that he did not even try to probe into the agent's background? The highly trance- or dissociation-prone person is far more likely to *assume* the value of a charismatic person based on some striking difference in appearance, rather than needing concrete evidence of that person's value.

Another important point is that, in the context of our discussion, value is something of importance to the person that the charismatic leader is trying to attract. Those of us in clinical roles know well that patients can develop attachments to us that go beyond a doctor-patient relationship because they greatly value what we contribute to their lives. Politicians know this and exploit it by using the catch phrases and citing the hot-button issues that attract blocs of voters. Cult leaders often provide a sense of belonging or differentiation that outcasts—or at least people who feel they are outcasts—desperately crave.

Inherent in this discussion of value is the notion that the charismatic leader is good at spotting the opportunity associated with providing that value. When a politician is speaking to union laborers who are currently out of work or underemployed, and he presents them with a plan for full employment, he's recognized opportunity and seized it.

In his instructions on recognizing opportunity, Hartley focuses on noticing evidence that the "follower" is available to the charm of the charismatic leader, and he specifically notes nonverbal language that imparts that availability: sharp visual focus, raised eyebrows, reaching out or moving closer, and so on. Interestingly, these features of human behavior are reminiscent of the portrayal of the hypnotic state in early literature, which focused on the intense fixed gaze of the hypnotized person and which referred to hypnosis as "animal magnetism." The spotlight is on a particular kind of person whose behavior signals special receptiveness to the charismatic approach, and once again, that person would be the Dionysian, highly trance-prone person.

"Grant an audience" is just another way of saying, "let the person get a little closer to you." Consider the behavioral patterns of many cult leaders in terms of this step: They often add a sexual component to the relationship. Hartley makes a very keen observation about the nature of charisma in this section; namely, too much familiarity with the charismatic person does indeed breed contempt. So effective charismatic persons draw others to them, but keep them at arm's length. Dionysian persons are more likely to stop at the snake oil booth at the county fair and allow themselves to be charmed into buying a bottle. Persons with a lesser trance-proneness (the Apollonians and Odysseans) are more likely to look for the list of ingredients.

If we follow the ploy of sexual favors through the next step of creating a sense of belonging, sex becomes a way of validating that the individual has made it to the inner circle. The important thing in continuing to build charisma is that the cult leader has to manage expectations, though, so the individual can't take the sexual dimension for granted or, as I suggested above, the leader's allure will be diminished. This part of the stratagem reminds us of the strong tendency of the highly trance-prone person to learn by affiliation. He is much more ready to "belong" without passing rational judgment on the person with whom he belongs. On the other hand, the extreme Apollonian is more likely to be a loner than a "belonger."

That moves us into the final step of differentiating the target. As part of the scheme, it makes sense that the leader would have multiple partners, perhaps determined by who "behaved" or even "excelled." Earning the privilege of sharing the cult leader's bed ten times a month might be like winning an Oscar in that context. Once differentiated, the leader can always up the ante: Today you sleep with me, tomorrow you follow me into the jungle.

The salient point is that the final step in the charismatic sequence is instilling in the other person a sense of her own unique value. Thus, we are charmed by those who leave us feeling valued. Certainly this was a stratagem deftly employed by Hitler, as he charmed a humiliated post–World War I nation into believing that in fact they were a superior race. But as we know, not every German citizen bought into their leader's propaganda.

As I mentioned in chapter 1, there are stories of children of abuse in which the children acted out or plunged into depression. For the trance-prone child like our little boy Joey, however, the outcome is dissociating to adapt. It is not a leap to assert that these are precisely the kind of people who are most likely to fall under the spell of a charismatic leader—one with good intentions or one with destructive impulses.

The steps just outlined comprise a path to manipulating certain kinds of people to redefine "normal" in their own lives. It's one approach to understanding how a person with a dissociative disorder adapts in an effort to feel normal.

Hartley concludes his discussion with the following:

> In summary, charisma is not some magical aura residing in the person at all. It is an ability to move others up [Maslow's] Hierarchy of Needs, quickly manipulating them to go from belonging to status. Ultimately, charisma is an effect living in the subject. And after all, as you leave them with the feeling of having known the x-iest (brightest, sexiest, wittiest) person alive you have given them some value and they can become more charismatic.[13]

I believe that Hartley's formulation of the charismatic effect is significantly strengthened when the dimension of dissociative potential of the audience is factored in. In other words, to be maximally effective, the persuasive effort would match the point on the Apollonian-Odyssean-Dionysian personality spectrum where the person being persuaded is found. That is, once the persuader has a notion about the personality style of the other, he can weight his persuasion more toward rational argument or more toward "charm." My hypothesis is that the best persuaders have a way of quickly sizing up the other person's style and rather automatically adapting their efforts to match. Perhaps Hartley is essentially agreeing with me in concluding, "Ultimately, charisma is an effect living in the subject."

The Uphill Trek to a Diagnosis

$\mathcal{A}$ny diagnosis a mental health professional makes is based on symptom presentation; that is, a certain combination of problems in behavior, thinking, feelings, and/or mood. That said, symptoms can be extremely deceiving. This always reminds me of an interlude in Shakespeare's play, *A Midsummer Night's Dream*. The poor weaver Nick Bottom, transformed by magic to have the head of an ass, becomes the object of the affection of Titania, Queen of the Fairies—also due to magic. "Symptoms" like Bottom's transformed head can distract us from the only truly useful questions, "What's *really* wrong?" and "How can we make it better?" Was Titania insane for falling in love with a man with the head of an ass? Or was she instead able to peer beneath his "symptom" to know the real Bottom?

A diagnostic process has to focus on the core person because, as the next chapter explores, symptoms can morph, deceive, and take clinicians off track just as they do the relatives, friends, and coworkers of the patient. So the fundamental question in the diagnostic encounter with the patient is, "Who are you?" As you come with me on this trek involving challenging diagnostic issues and see in the case study of Dr. Saroj Parida how they play out, consider this: to achieve a truly useful diagnostic understanding of the patient, a mental health professional needs to be just as aware of the temperament, intellect, talents, social support network, and trance capacity of the person as of his life history, current complaints, and hopes and dreams for the future.

In other words, who's the man behind the donkey head? In the case of Saroj Parida, the story is one of a man whose natural capacity for mind wandering became the path to a certain type of rarely seen mental disorder in which he had many "heads."

NAMING THE ILLNESS

Many years ago, a friend of mine was reading the back of an aspirin bottle: "Headache, toothache, neuralgia—what the heck is neuralgia?" We laughed because, at the time, neither of us had a clue, and we figured that a lot of other people who took aspirin didn't either. If you didn't feel quite right and all you had was a bottle of aspirin, with hopes of feeling better you might conclude from the process of elimination that you had neuralgia, since you didn't have a headache, toothache, or any of the other aches listed on the bottle.

Unfortunately, a person who is unusual in appearance or behavior often receives a lay "diagnosis" of crazy. People around him go through a mental checklist analogous to the list on the aspirin bottle: He's not on drugs, suffering from a visible injury, or in any danger, so he must be crazy. The big cultural difference between the diagnoses of "neuralgia" and "crazy," of course, is that the latter is pejorative and stigmatizing.

As a psychiatrist, I see patients who have carried that ersatz diagnosis around for years and let it warp their self-perception as well as give rise to some serious and sometimes avoidable psychological complications such as depression and substance abuse. Instead of receiving targeted treatment for post-traumatic stress syndrome or bipolar disorder, for example, they find themselves on medication for a sleep disorder or schizophrenia.

One fundamental challenge in diagnosing, therefore, is that the patient himself often doesn't know what's really wrong with him, assumes that he's "crazy," and is either too ashamed to seek help or doesn't know where to look for it. And then, to compound the confusion, friends and family make assumptions based on symptoms. Their recommended "treatments" could involve St. John's wort, a shot of brandy, or a gluten-free diet. Those things may not hurt, but they probably won't solve the problem, either.

Once that patient gets to the "right" clinician, diagnostic challenges still remain. The public expects diagnostic clarity and accuracy from the psychiatric community. As so poignantly illustrated by Dr. David Spiegel's research with the veterans whose chronic post-traumatic stress symptoms were erroneously diagnosed, clinicians don't always meet that expectation. In fairness to mental health practitioners, diagnosis is sometimes made very difficult for at least these reasons. First, individuals with different personality types will respond to extreme life stresses differently. Secondly, very different disorders can appear to be virtually identical in terms of symptoms. For example, persons who are sleep deprived for an extended period of time will begin to look indistinguishable from persons with paranoid schizophrenia, complete with paranoid beliefs and hallucinations. With the restoration of sleep, the "schizophrenia" goes away.

Take a look at the two ways that people might respond to trauma: Those more prone to trance—like frequent daydreamers—are more likely to dissociate after trauma than those with a naturally low trance capacity. People in the latter group are likely either to act out their emotional reaction to the trauma or plunge into depression.

Those people who are more likely to dissociate may end up with persisting dissociative disorders as a result of psychic trauma. But then again, the trance-prone people suffering from other kinds of mental illness unrelated to a history of trauma are, nevertheless, still more likely to dissociate problematically. Related to that is the point that dissociative states can resemble psychotic states, which are a different phenomenon with different causes and a different neurobiology to them, and which require a different treatment approach.

In short, the process of distinguishing dissociative symptoms from others and making an accurate diagnosis might take weeks or months of ongoing, careful observation and evaluation.

While brain imaging occasionally plays a role in clarifying the nature of mental symptoms, it is of no value currently in helping to diagnose any of the dissociative disorders. While research in this area is ongoing and beginning to observe differences in brain appearance with different types of dissociation, we are likely many years away from practical use of brain imaging studies as a means of aiding diagnosis of dissociative disorder.

DIAGNOSTIC TOOLS—NEUROBIOLOGY

Apart from Alzheimer's disease or non-Alzheimer's dementing illnesses, for which we are routinely using brain imaging to see the evidence of an organic problem, the psychiatric community generally does not rely on these tests to confirm or reject a diagnosis. Even in those cases, the diagnosis stems primarily from clinical presentation and history. The imaging studies we have at our disposal can occasionally be helpful in ruling out physical causes of psychiatric symptoms, such as brain tumors, stroke, or seizures (for which electroencephalograms [EEGs] are useful).

When we do brain imaging studies with people who have different types of disorders such as DID, their main value is to provide interesting neurophysiological correlations. But that does not mean these studies are of any practical value clinically. This brings to mind a serious flaw in current medical journalism. I saw a headline recently that asserted that brain imaging could make an autism diagnosis. This is a far cry from reality, as captured in a more responsible headline about the same study: "Brain Imaging May Improve Autism Diagnosis."[1] The study addressed the fact that some correlations are being made in brain imaging studies with symptoms of autism, specifically language impairment; that does not even suggest a clinician could use the imaging result to make a diagnosis of autism.

What's the harm? The parent of a child with a diagnosis of autism "shops around" for a doctor who will subject her child to very expensive imaging studies (which in themselves can have potential to harm the patient due to the nature of imaging technology) because she's desperately seeking evidence that either confirms or rejects the unpleasant diagnosis. Regardless of what information the study reveals—whether the tests seem to support the diagnosis or bring it into question—the child still presents as autistic, so what's the physician supposed to do? Treat for autism, of course. In short, the tests might deepen understanding of what's going on inside the child's head, but at least at the moment, they do not in the slightest affect diagnosis or treatment, and instead represent a waste of money and medical resources. I wish such examples of sensationalistic medical journalism were infrequent, but they are dismayingly common. Remember the early 1980s, when we were cautioned that anyone who ate more than one egg per week was going to clog his coronary arteries with cholesterol?

When it comes to aiding victims of trauma who are dissociating, we have a very similar circumstance as with autism. The studies don't determine the treatment, but in research settings they are beginning to show promise in identifying brain effects of successful treatment. These studies, then, may someday point to modifications in treatment approach.

For example, as I mentioned briefly in chapter 2, the body releases neurochemicals in response to stress. In some cases of extreme stress, there is an excessive release of stress hormones that affect areas of the brain that are key players in *integrative functions*. This phrase takes us all the way back to the French psychologist Pierre Janet, credited with first using the term "dissociation" in the late nineteenth century. Janet posited that integration reflects the ability of a brain to execute a sequence of actions and that a critical component of integration is *personification*. You probably know the term "personification" as a literary term. Phrases like "snowflakes dancing" and "anger raising its ugly head" are examples of it, meaning that the author has brought something nonhuman into the realm of the human, since snowflakes can't dance and anger has no head. That's a good starting point for understanding the use of the term in a psychiatric context. Traumatized people who remain capable of the act of personification are able to maintain their memory of the traumatic event as part of their "personal" history, rather than sticking the memory of the event somewhere deep and inaccessible within their unconscious mind—that is, "dissociating" it. The authors of a recent study on how people handle trauma after the fact explain the impact of not being able to do that: "When personification fails, the development of a coherent sense of personal existence in a framework of the past, the present, and the future is compromised."[2] In other words, gaps in our memory of past experience predispose us to gaps in the way we anticipate the future. In fact, gaps created by dissociated memories of traumatic experiences tend to cause us to assume that the future will inevitably be filled with more traumatic experiences.

The authors of this study go on to say that the difficulty that some people have with personifying horrible events in their life has a biological basis. Those neurochemicals released at the time of trauma can shrink a deep brain structure called the hippocampus, for example. The hippocampus has a big responsibility for moving short-term memory into long-term memory. (Not surprisingly, it's one of the first areas of the brain to suffer damage from Alzheimer's disease.) The good news is that a study based on magnetic resonance imaging (MRI) conducted by an international team including researchers from the National Institute of Mental Health and Yale University School of Medicine indicates that successful trauma treatment can reverse the process, so that the hippocampus of some PTSD sufferers has approximated a more normal size.[3]

With all of this accumulating knowledge of brain chemicals and brain activity, you may well be skeptical about my opening statement that imaging studies are not used to either confirm or deny a diagnosis of a dissociative disorder. Now let me ratchet up that skepticism even more.

The lead author of the study with PTSD sufferers, as well as another colleague who participated in it, conducted another MRI-based study on patients with DID. Eric Vermetten of the Rudolf Magnus Institute of Neurosciences in The Netherlands, and J. Douglas Bremner of the Emory University School of Medicine in Atlanta, were among the researchers who studied fifteen patients with DID and compared the results with twenty-three healthy subjects.[4] Their conclusion: the patients with DID had a smaller hippocampus and amygdala than the healthy patients. The amygdala has the job of remembering and processing emotional reactions.

Even with the weight of these studies, we still cannot say that imaging confirms a diagnosis of DID or any other dissociative disorder. These results give us key insights into the correlations between brain activity and brain structures with a particular condition, but we must still ask ourselves two questions about what the data tell us.

1. This is a great start, but what are we yet missing? With all of the things going on in our amazing brains, what other actions, interactions, and reactions that are vital to our understanding are going undetected by current science?
2. Are we dealing with a chicken-egg situation? Did the trauma victims in the study start out life with a smaller-than-normal hippocampus and/or amygdala, thereby predisposing them to dissociative episodes?

It is questions such as these that keep us coming to back to a deep appreciation for the neurobiological tools in the diagnostic process, but not an everyday clinical reliance on them, when it comes to trauma-induced dissociation.

DIAGNOSTIC TOOLS—PSYCHOLOGY

In using standardized psychological tests responsibly to aid in psychiatric diagnosis, clinicians are bound by the rules of interpretation of the tests. And even though a psychologist administers the Minnesota Multiphasic Personality Inventory (MMPI)—one of the most frequently relied-on tests in mental health—the test involving all true-false answers is machine scored, so it leaves virtually no room for the clinician to put a spin on the results. A test like the picture-based Thematic Apperception Test (TAT) is not machine scored, but there are still rigorous guidelines to interpreting regarding the meaning of responses.

Another key point is that these objective psychological tests need to be taken and interpreted in the immediate context in which the test was done. In Saroj's case—and the significance of this will become clearer in the next section on DID diagnosis—it was presumably the host personality who took the tests. Therefore, some of the results do not jibe with behavior described by his wife and friends.

This calls up an interesting question: Can an alter take a psychological test? If so, what does it tell us? Researchers conducting tests with patients with DID determined that a memory test had been taken by a person in an altered state.[5] They subsequently gave a different alter of the same host a memory test. Repeating the process with the alters and the host, they attempted to determine whether or not the alters were amnestic for the memory test they conducted with other alters. They found the memory was intact for information given in different altered states. While the results certainly provide useful insights into the interrelationships of alters in terms of memory, the researchers had to conclude that memory tests would not, therefore, be useful in determining the presence of DID. However, neither could they logically conclude that they had found a disproof of the validity of the diagnosis, as it is accepted that the amnesia between alters and host is selective and often partial.

There are dozens of personality tests, most not nearly as sophisticated and reliable as MMPI, that a psychologist might administer to help ascertain a diagnosis. There are also psychological tests such as the Rorschach Test and TAT that use images instead of questions or statements to help the psychologist determine a subject's mental and emotional state. Like MMPI, TAT is among the most widely used tests of its type.

The TAT is a useful projective technique that has been in use since the 1930s. The subject is presented with a series of picture cards and instructed to create a story based on each picture. The story should have a beginning, middle, and ending, stressing what each character is thinking and feeling. The subject will "project" into his story the important emotional issues in his life, some of which lie beyond his conscious awareness. In this fashion, projective tests are a wonderful way to obtain reliable clues as to troubling features of a patient's mind without upsetting the patient. The point of the TAT is to help unearth hopes, fears, or perception of current reality.

The MMPI is an objective technique, as opposed to a projective one like the TAT. The original MMPI debuted in 1939, but MMPI-2, which is what we now use, was released in 1989. It has 567 items to which the subject responds with "true" or "false." The results give insights into personality structure and psychopathology. In terms of personality structure, we can see how certain types of people have certain characteristics in common. For example, MMPI data show that lawyers, policemen, and criminals as a group tend to share some important personality traits. This helps us to understand why policemen and prosecutors can be so unusually good at what they do. In terms of psychopathology, the MMPI can provide key insights on such things as acute anxiety state, depressed suicidal ideation, threatened assault, situational stress, mental confusion, and persecutory ideas.

THE DID DIAGNOSIS

A thorough psychiatric diagnosis involves five parts, or axes.

- Axis I is the DSM-IV descriptive diagnosis, for example, "major depression," "bipolar disorder," "schizophrenia," and so on.

- Axis II characterizes the personality, so if there is a personality disorder diagnosis, it would go in this category.

In the DSM, personality disorders are sorted into three categories: cluster A, cluster B, and cluster C. *Cluster A* includes schizoid, schizotypal, and paranoid personalities. These are the most potentially disabling personality disorders, whose sufferers can at times experience significant breaks with reality. A schizoid person has a lot going on internally in terms of a fantasy life, but avoids normal social interaction and doesn't enjoy it. Schizotypal personalities are marked by extreme social awkwardness and the presence of unusual beliefs and behavioral oddities. Of course, the hallmark of a paranoid personality is unremitting suspiciousness of all others. *Cluster B* personalities tend to be less impaired than cluster A, albeit still seriously handicapping to the sufferer as well as to those with whom they interact. They are the borderline personalities, narcissistic personalities, and antisocial personalities. *Cluster C* represents the healthiest of the personality disorders, including avoidance, passive-aggressive, obsessive-compulsive, and others. They are higher functioning than the others. (Note that dissociative identity disorder is not classified as a personality disorder. Rather, it is included in the section of the DSM-IV entitled "Dissociative Disorders.")

An article in *Psychiatry* called "Dissociative Amnesia and DSM-IV-TR Cluster C Personality Traits" supports a surprising hypothesis that I've held to for quite a while; namely, that cluster C types are more prone than cluster B to dissociative amnesia—and I suspect, they are more prone to the full range of dissociative disorders. Researchers found that some dissociative amnesia appears in cluster B types, but it's found a lot more frequently in the cluster C types. Conclusion: we find more dissociative disorders in the more highly integrated personalities.[6]

- Axis III includes physical diagnoses, especially those that could have significant implications for the person's Axis I and II diagnoses. If a person had coronary artery disease, for example, we would list it here.
- Axis IV lists psychosocial stressors, that is, any current or historical environmental circumstances that bear upon the person's mental illness. Severe marital issues or a disabled child are two examples of factors that would fit this category.
- Axis V refers to global assessment of functioning (GAF). It's a numerical score, from 1 to 99, which indicates how well the person is doing in the world. Clinicians are encouraged to give two GAF scores, one of which gives a current GAF and one offering a sense of the highest level reached during the previous twelve months.

My notes covering our first emergency session on March 6, 2009, stated the following in terms of the five axes:

Axis I: Post-traumatic stress disorder, chronic vs. delayed
            R/O dissociative identity disorder
            R/O narcolepsy
            R/O malingering
Axis II: Diagnosis deferred
Axis III: R/O organic brain pathology
Axis IV: Psychosocial stressors: unresolved childhood trauma; loss of
            employment under retraumatizing circumstances; recent raid
            of house by authorities and subsequent arrest
Axis V: Current GAF: 30

A few days later, I added "bipolar disorder or major depression with melancholia" to the list of Axis I possibilities. As Saroj shared more detail about the frenetic, chaotic insurance billings, usually occurring in the wee hours of the morning, I wondered whether he was suffering from the fever-pitched madness of a manic mood swing. After all, at the peak of mania, sufferers can become so delusional as to believe that cranking out invoices and stuffing them at random into mailing envelopes is a perfectly logical thing to do.

PTSD was the *provisional diagnosis*, that is, a working diagnosis; it was provisional because there were other possibilities that needed to be either validated or ruled out. Inserting *R/O*, or rule out, indicates that my next steps would involve tests, evaluation, and observation to either rule out those diagnoses or give them more weight. Narcolepsy is a neurological disorder whose cardinal symptom is irresistible daytime sleep attacks, but which is usually accompanied by various disturbances in nighttime sleep and it can cause a number of other symptoms such as hallucinations.[7] Malingering is just a fancy medical way of saying that the patient is faking symptoms to achieve some objective of which the patient is consciously aware.

I feel it important to focus briefly on the concept of a *malingering disorder* and distinguish it from two related, but also radically different, disorders: conversion and factitious disorders. In malingering, the motive for "symptom" production is conscious to the person. A person who fakes back pain to collect worker's compensation fits into this category. By nature, malingering is a sociopathic act permitted by a defective conscience. In a *factitious disorder*, the symptom is consciously generated, but the motive for it is unconscious to the person. For example, when I was a resident, there was a girl in the hospital who had "fevers of unknown origin," or "FUO" (medical personnel are abbreviation addicts). She kept spiking these fevers and no one could tell where they were coming from. That is, until one day a nurse found her in the bathroom loading up a syringe with toilet water after she'd had a bowel movement. She was therefore consciously injecting herself with fecal fluid, but the reasons she did it were unconscious to her until later uncovered in the course of psychiatric consultation. The third category of disorders on this spectrum is the *conversion disorder*. In this situation, both the production of the symptoms and the motivation are unconscious to the patient. An instance of this was the man who woke up one morning with hysterical paralysis of his right arm. He was not consciously producing the symptom; all he knew is that he couldn't move his right arm. There was no physical reason for the symptom, but with psychotherapeutic treatment, he eventually realized that he was enraged with his father and had fantasies of taking a hammer and bashing in his father's head. He's a right handed person, so one day he woke up and his right arm was paralyzed, which saved him from acting out his rage in a way his conscience found unacceptable. The psychotherapy allowed for suitable resolution of his anger and therefore a "cure" for his paralysis.

You can readily see a relationship between a conversion disorder and dissociative identity disorder. In the example of the conversation disorder I described, the consciousness is dissociated from that part of the motor system that controls the movement of the right arm. DID is the mental version of this physical phenomenon. In both cases, the sufferer is dissociated from intolerably frightening emotions in order to meet the demands of conscience or safety. You may also recognize the disservice we can potentially do to patients by misdiagnosing them as malingering if in fact they are fundamentally not in control of their symptoms and unaware of the meaning and purpose of them. And you can also see why competent psychiatric diagnosis sometimes is a painstaking and time-consuming process.

Among the recommendations I recorded that first day with Saroj were psychological testing—with the projective TAT test I referred to above being the most telling about malingering—along with a physical examination that would include brain imaging studies and certain laboratory studies, and referral to a sleep disorders clinic.

After the sleep study on April 8, I ruled out narcolepsy, but the study revealed that Saroj suffered from sleep apnea, a condition involving unrefreshing sleep that can have many different causes. Part of Saroj's daytime fatigue and confusion undoubtedly resulted from it, and he found relief through the use of a CPAP (Continuous Positive Airway Pressure) machine at night.

Brain imaging revealed no abnormalities, so I could rule out structural brain lesions or other organic issues as a cause for his aberrant behavior.

On April 16, Saroj had his psychological tests, which were very telling. When a psychiatrist refers a patient to a psychologist for projective testing, the testing clinician asks, "What are you looking for?" In Saroj's case, I simply said that I was concerned my patient was dissociating. I didn't want to influence the process in any way by even suggesting that I suspected Saroj had DID. Dr. Michael S. Greevy, a psychologist I'd worked with many times before, used TAT and MMPI with Saroj.

For the TAT, Greevy gave him a series of cards, one at a time. In each case, the content below presents Saroj's answers verbatim, followed by a summary of suggested themes offered by Greevy.[8] As you read these, keep in mind that the style of the response—somewhat rambling, sometimes oddly specific—is not uncommon when a person has the task of looking at a picture and being asked to create a story about what the picture conveys. Maryann does an exercise similar to this in her body language classes to teach people the effect of projection on reading body language. She has found that the identical photograph can produce wildly different interpretations of what the body positions in the photos mean. People in the class are always amazed at how powerful projection really is; the interpretations are so different because each person has a slightly different way of projecting his or her own experiences, perspective, habits, and feelings onto the picture.

Several abbreviations are used in the notes below, namely, WF or WT (what is he feeling or thinking?); HTO (how does the story turn out?); VLP (very long pause). Greevy describes frequently recurring themes following each of Saroj's descriptions of the "story on the card."

> **Card 1**: A young boy sitting in front of and looking at a picture of something or writing, concentrating engrossed in part, sitting on a chair (WT) picture or writing. I do not think he is drawing or writing. He does not have a pencil, seems a little sad by the expression in his eyes looking downward hand on his cheek, left one on his left ear, possible sad looking at whatever it is—what he might be sad about at that age eight to ten years old, maybe a picture of an animal, a dog or something that he loves and might be injured he's feeling sad. (HTO) In his mind he's hoping his favorite pet will get better with time and how to provide help for the animal. His mind thinks if his parents are aware of the situation, if not, he'll bring it to their attention so that they can take care of the suffering animal. I'm not sure of the outcome. I don't know the extent of the injury. There's a sense of urgency that needs to be taken care of quickly by the doctor or surgeon. I wonder if he did anything to harm his pet unknowingly he's sadder so there's a sense of urgency to make the situation better. He also wonders if it was an accident or something deliberate that was done. His first thought was if he did something unknowingly or if he is responsible or neglected the pet so it got in trouble. He feels the need to do something about it hoping from the bottom of his heart that the animal recovers.

Card 1 themes: Mood: sad. Urgency, caused harm, blame, responsibility, unknowingly neglect, hope for outcome, fear of loss over wrongdoing.

Before moving through the rest of the selected results, I want to give some additional insights into the administration and meaning of the TAT. A popular, lay term for the test is the "picture interpretation technique." The pictures are deliberately both provocative and ambiguous. Unlike the MMPI, which is administered to people who are at least eighteen years old, the TAT is often used with children. There may be as many as twenty cards used, but generally psychologists use a smaller number that they feel are likely to elicit the most useful information about the person's feelings and state of mind.

Here are a three more examples of how Saroj responded that give fascinating insights into his preoccupations and emotional state:

Card 5: A lady with a door half open looking into the room; there's someone beyond the picture who seems to be a little angry and ready to close the door, talking with the individual [is] a child who may have done something wrong in the process of scolding him. What he did was not correct, he needs to be punished. She is laying out the punishment by closing the door; the child's protesting: punish me but don't leave me in the room alone, but she's giving punishment directions. The child is feeling very scared about being in the room alone. The mother's about to close the door. He's afraid maybe to kneel down facing the wall (he demonstrates) he was told to kneel and hold his ears as part of the punishment he's scared of being in the room alone. He's facing the wall requesting to keep the door half open or open it farther. She doesn't seem to be in agreement with that. The thoughts through the child's mind is if life is worthwhile, a combination of feeling alone scared and worthless at the same time (HTO). He thinks of the love his mother has for him and feeling that love maybe she's teaching me her way of reacting to the situation but behind it all she has unconditional love. Though now feeling worthless, she and father have love and he—she has put up with this situation now and will become braver and stronger, a better person, after this. He heard the parents, if you do something wrong they have to point it out to not repeat it and be better after that.

Card 5 themes: Others are angry, blame, responsibility, punishment, did wrong, become a better/stronger person hope, fear of abandonment because of wrongdoing, scared, alone, worthless, questioning if life is worthwhile.

Card 17 BM: (VLP) A picture of an athletic male, youngish who looks to be naked seems like he's climbing by holding on to a rope looking at somebody or something. His expression doesn't look very sad even though it's a rope. He's not sure he wants to hang himself on it; it's difficult to do in that position. It could also be that he has a female partner not in the picture and he's showing her how athletic and strong he is by climbing on the rope. He's trying to show her his masculinity to see if that maybe arouses her or something. A part of the rope looks like it's going between his legs in the genital area. Maybe he's trying to tell her she could do the same if she gets naked looking at him and doing what he is doing. Thoughts, if he sees her naked he will get aroused and they will have sex or something, I'm not sure if the rope is for some sort of foreplay or something like that.

Card 17 BM themes: Suicide, sexual preoccupation.

Card 13 B: It looks like a young child sitting at an entrance, a barn or something; doesn't look like an entry to a house, barn or outside. Doesn't have any shoes; if that was an accidental thing . . . chin on his hands, hands clasped and chin resting; sad about something. He feels all alone at the front step of a big opening inside of this is very dark, could be something happened in the main house and he ran outside; something was making him very sad and he wanted to get away, maybe his favorite place. He didn't want to run away completely to get away from something to sit by himself and think about what happened. Something, don't know how he ends up there, something he does to avoid something, his body takes him there and almost automatically because he's done so many times—an automatic escape route. Maybe it's horses or animals that take his mind away from something else that is going on so he comes and sits there to get some solace and peace. His eyes are squinted because the bright sunlight on the outside. He realizes this, he has a tendency to do this automatically, get a little scared because he'd rather know where he is going rather than it being unknown after he sits there a while he feels more at ease, he goes back, this is a safe haven he has created for himself.

Dr. Greevy looked at all the responses and distilled the themes running through them, with Saroj's take on Card 13 B being a fairly obvious suggestion of possible dissociation. His summary is as follows:

The primary mood tone of Dr. Parida's stories is sadness over feared loss, rejection and abandonment over some wrongdoing. The characters in many of his stories feel alone, scared and worthless. They question if life is worthwhile and consider suicide. However, there is an associated theme of hope that events will turn out okay; there will be a positive outcome, and that family and friends will return and he will become a better, stronger person. The wrongdoings are typically described as accidental, a mistake or done unknowingly. There is a strong desire for closeness and intimacy, both emotionally and physically. Dr. Parida also referred to an uncovering of the past and a change in mental status. Dr. Parida's last story (Card 13 B) is about a boy that has developed an automatic escape route and safe haven to feel something sad that happens many times in the "main house." This escape scares him "because he'd rather know where he is going rather than it being unknown"—a seemingly clear reference to the process of dissociation.

In reviewing the answers that Saroj gave on the MMPI, a few things stand out as extremely odd—things that would seem consistent with a condition of mental illness if someone had no background on him. For example, in responding "true" or "false" to the statement "I have a good appetite," Saroj responded with an F. The response supports a supposition that he's in an acute anxiety state or depressed, and in fact, it is a correct response for the host personality we know as Saroj. In reality, as Saroj's wife verified, he often ate unseemly amounts of food. We recognized later that how much he ate and what he ate depended on which alter happened to be at the forefront of activity. Another oddity was his T response to "I find it hard to keep my mind on a task or job." When Saroj took the test, there was no official diagnosis of DID, but what I did know was that he had many hours of continuous activity doing fraudulent billing, had a reputation for extraordinary focus in caring for critically ill infants, and was known on the golf course for having an unusual ability to stay "in the zone." The psychologist would not be in a position to read anything into test results like that, but having already completed eighteen sessions with him, one of which included his wife, I took particular note of some of these incongruous responses.

These disconnections illustrate that conscious awareness and unconscious motivations and feelings are two different things. Saroj might have a ravenous appetite unconsciously, but feel as though he has no appetite at all; his eating behavior would not match his conscious sensory experience of hunger or appetite.

So the ultimate question is: What is the person consciously aware of? We're learning all the time, even when we're not consciously aware that we're learning. We're experiencing all the time, even when we're not consciously aware that we're experiencing. A pedestrian example of that lack of conscious awareness is what's commonly referred to as "highway hypnosis." A driver can see an exit sign, yet not be consciously aware of it and drive right past it. As far as the conscious mind is concerned, the exit sign never came into view. This simple illustration captures the essence of dissociative identity disorder, as well as dissociative experiences in general.

With the results of neurological and psychological testing in hand, and with the benefit of a thorough medical and developmental history and ample direct clinical experience with the patient, the clinician is finally in a position to make a definitive judgment as to whether the patient is suffering from dissociative identity disorder instead of or in addition to other psychiatric diagnoses. (A person may have mood and/or anxiety disorders in addition to DID.) In other words, the diagnosis is ultimately made based on a careful history and direct clinical observation over a sufficient number of therapy sessions. The testing for "rule outs" is in the name of diagnostic thoroughness. At any rate, such a relatively rare and complex diagnosis as DID should never be cavalierly made.

In the case of Saroj, that diagnostic process took four months.

I had first seen him on an urgent basis on a Thursday, and my next meeting with him was the following day to complete the history taking and mental state evaluation. Right after that, I called his attorney who was convinced that Saroj had a grandiose, narcissistic personality and figured he could just get away with fraud. I imagine he imparted this bias to Saroj (remember the discussion about mistaking malingering), because Saroj promptly sought another attorney. I spoke with his replacement, Gavin Lentz, the following Tuesday and he gave me the same story: "I've seen a million of these cases! These guys are so smart, they think they can get away with anything!" Gavin soon gained a different impression, however. As soon as he got to know his client, he saw what I saw: a very, very sick man whose chief complaint, voiced in our second session, was "I'm so confused about what I've been doing these past two years. I must have lost my mind."

As the treatment progressed I discovered that Saroj's childhood was rife with a number of different types of trauma from infancy through the age of twelve; that raised the index of suspicion that he might have a dissociative disorder. Then there were dissociative episodes that I witnessed here at his treatment sessions. The first occurred within the first month of treatment. In one, I found him sitting in the waiting room with a glazed look in his eyes, speaking in a language unrecognizable—presumably Indian—to me. Some of the episodes were even more bizarre.

As I mentioned earlier, I once found him lying outside the office on snow-covered grass. He held a fetal position and would not move. Gently, slowly—and all the while referring to him as Saroj rather the name of an alter—I aroused him from the dissociated state. Usually when I would call his name, he would come out of the dissociated state and return to his core personality; at that point, we could go on with treatment.

His history and interactions during therapy, including the dissociative episodes I witnessed, gave me the content I needed to advance my thinking toward a diagnosis of DID. One thing was abundantly clear: Saroj proved to be highly trance-prone—clearly a Dionysian. According to the Spiegels, when people at that end of the trance spectrum develop psychiatric disorders, they are particularly prone to developing dissociative disorders and, interestingly enough, also bipolar disorders. One thing that clinicians need to consider in a situation like Saroj's, therefore, is the possibility of *comorbidity*, that is, that he lives with both a dissociative disorder and a bipolar disorder. Short of outright bipolar disorder, some persons by nature are what some researchers would refer to as *hyperthymic*, that is, characterized by a wellspring of physical and mental energy and an inordinately high activity level.

This phenomenon of a hyperthymic temperament points to one of the many reasons why an in-depth patient history plays a profound role in diagnosis. Saroj has childhood memories such as his brother chasing him down the street, threatening to throttle him with a steel rod. Was Saroj such a mischievous, hyperactive kid that he bothered his brother to the point where he wanted to just shut him up? He also remembers his father lining up the kids to administer punishment at the same time. As his father prepared to spank him, Saroj would laugh, so he would get spanked even harder. Incidents like this pepper his early memories, leading me to wonder, by dint of his exuberance as a kid, how much trouble did he bring on? A hyperthymic person of any age could annoy people around him to the point where he, in a sense, invites trauma. Certainly it's true that Saroj has memories throughout his life of hyped-up performance that wasn't often met with admiration or gratitude. On one hand, he could work tirelessly to save the life of a baby when fellow clinicians considered the case hopeless, gave up and left. On the other hand, his persistence could at times understandably annoy hospital staff to the point that they wanted to push him out a window.[9] In short, there are times when the person might be better able to contain or to channel the energy than others, so once again, people around the individual can make excuses for the bursts of eccentricity while they appreciate the positive results of the person's charged-up behavior.

Over time, many historical details suggested that Saroj was *not* simply bipolar and manifesting a narcissistic personality. For example, an intelligent neonatologist—someone acknowledged as a genius at an early age—would not bill for a multi-day sleep study for a tiny baby. Billing an insurance company for putting a critically ill infant in a sleep study goes beyond absurd, even for a delusional bipolar individual. Further, a brilliant guy with a narcissistic personality is going to be so enamored over his cleverness that he would not submit such a blatantly ridiculous claim, even if he believed he were too Teflon-coated to get caught.

So after four months of sessions and exhaustive testing, no doubt remained in my mind: Saroj had DID.

GETTING IT WRONG

As in the case of the veterans with PTSD who were misdiagnosed with schizophrenia, the results of getting it wrong are horrifying. Those veterans lost years of their life confined to a hospital, medicated heavily for an illness they didn't have. The medication itself can cause neurological side effects that are permanent. The collateral costs are social—disconnection from loved ones—as well as both financial, because they are prevented from earning a living, and emotional in terms of an erosion of self-respect.

In Saroj's case, a misdiagnosis could have resulted in a suicidal act. Many times in the course of his treatment, Saroj reached the point of driving his car to the edge of a quarry located near his house, contemplating suicide. This behavior ironically began to occur after he began to integrate. That is, as he began to endure negative emotions—anger, terror, and other extreme emotions—that were previously sequestered out of conscious feeling into alters, they so unsettled him that he contemplated the most complete and permanent escape of all. Fortunately, he invariably called me and gave me the chance to restore his hope that ultimately he could emerge from the quagmire of his current life. Had his psychiatrist not understood the nature of dissociation, the protective function of the alters, and Saroj's increased risk of self-harm as he began the process of integration—or even more, had Saroj been in a system of care wherein he would have had to deal with an on-call therapist with little or no familiarity with his case—he realistically might not have survived.

This is just a salient example of a prevalent reality in contemporary mental health care in our culture regarding persons with dissociative disorders: they must be properly diagnosed, but just as importantly, they need to be properly understood and treated. And finally, persons with dissociative disorders and their almost certain traumatic history must have a particularly intense and trusting relationship with an empathic and available therapist.

· *6* ·

Treating the Symptoms:
Everyone's Nightmare

*W*ithout a doubt, Adolf Hitler had symptoms of a personality disorder, but his doctor treated him for something completely different: hypochondria. As part of supposed treatment, Hitler absorbed various toxic substances, which would only have exacerbated both his hypochondria and his personality disorder.

The hypochondriac belief that "there's something wrong with me and no one seems to be able to figure out what it is" is consistent with the developmental dynamic of the narcissistic personality. At their unconscious core, persons with narcissistic personality disorder feel there is something seriously wrong with them, and the defense that becomes the hallmark of their conscious personality is "There is *nothing* wrong with me; in fact, I'm perfect. The problem is the rest of the world." (Here's an ironic historical tidbit: The German word for defenses that have made their way into the person's personality style is *charakterpanzerung*, which translates to "character armor." Of course, the tank division in Hitler's army was called the Panzer division.) So whenever narcissistic personalities feel discomfort, when things aren't going their way, it certainly isn't because they erred or they had any measure of incompetence. The problem is that the flawed world into which they had the misfortune of being born is not treating them the way they deserve to be treated. In short, if there is any case in history of how treating the symptoms and not the illness becomes everyone's nightmare, it is the case of Hitler.

Contrast cases such as Hitler's with that of Saroj Parida, who has treatment for his core illness. First of all, Saroj had a seeming narcissistic demeanor that others regularly found off-putting. This feature did not represent true narcissism but instead what some have called "pseudo-narcissism"; that is, in Saroj's case the personality "leftovers" when so many elements of his

85

thinking and feeling self were hidden away in various alters. He would try to conceal his ever-present feeling of being an imposter by presenting himself as ultra-competent. The true narcissist is consciously unaware of his deep core fear of inadequacy. I see this feature diminishing in Saroj as he integrates. His narcissism was nurtured by parents and teachers who praised his artistic and mathematical genius from an early age; all of that success occurred concurrently with the abuse that provoked his DID. As time goes on and Saroj progresses toward mental health, he becomes more empathetically attuned while the pseudo-narcissism recedes.

Now recall in chapter 4 that I mentioned those doctors at a dinner party who "diagnosed" Saroj. Their focus was solely on the symptom of narcissism. They didn't see it as the tip of the iceberg; they saw it as the iceberg.

People respond to symptoms, whether they are health professionals or those around the individual exhibiting problems: "You seem depressed." "He beat that child—he's evil!" "You didn't hear a word I said, did you?" Similarly, the person with the symptoms is often the first to jump to conclusions about what might cure or mitigate the sense of abnormality.

THE RABBIT HOLE OF FACT FINDING

The trap that lures friends and family—and perhaps even some mental health professionals—into treating the symptoms often relates to the desire for "the truth," or the mistaken belief that all relevant facts regarding verifiable history of trauma must be on the table in order for therapy to be successful. Or judgments on the best way to proceed are based simply on empirical evidence: what the person says and how the person acts. Add to that the projections that we all tend to make about the meaning of words and actions, and the result can be a view of "what's best for her" that's as ridiculous as telling patients with the bubonic plague in the Middle Ages that confessing their sins would cure them.

The truth will not necessarily set you free; ironically, the search for it may plunge you straight into the nonsense of the rabbit hole.

Psychiatrist Richard Kluft, a renowned DID expert, stresses a very important point time and time again: When we encounter patients, we are dealing with life as *they* have experienced it and now remember it. In that sense, as we go about helping to heal the person, what actually literally happened in the person's life is fundamentally irrelevant unless it has forensic implications, that is, legal authorities need to ascertain whether the trauma involved prosecutable criminal behavior and/or perpetrators must be restrained from further abuse.

Those of us who provide therapy to trauma patients with dissociative conditions are supposed to know that and let go of our urge to know the literal "truth" of the patient's past and trauma. But people who are not clinicians follow the normal, human tendency to assume that one must have the facts. And unless the individual offering the information *decides* to lie, what comes out of his mouth will either be the literal truth or the product of a demented or crazy mind. Let's take a look at some background on why that just isn't so.

In chapter 4, I referenced three types of dissociation, with Type 1 involving a sense of reliving a trauma, not just remembering it. Using the nomenclature of Charles S. Myers, a consulting psychologist to the British armies in France during the First World War, this type of dissociation is associated with an "emotional" personality, or EP. In 1940, Myers published a classic book called *Shell Shock in France, 1914–1918: Based on a War Diary*. In that work, he laid a foundation for discussing dissociation as it is affected by one's *premorbid personality*, that is, a state before the onset of mental illness. His idea was that those soldiers he studied had a kind of divided personality—the "apparently normal" personality (ANP) and the emotional one.[1]

Myers' insights helped to lay the groundwork for modern understandings of how persons with a high dissociative potential will tend to remember a traumatic event in a fragmented rather than coherent way. Thus, the person with trauma-induced dissociation can legitimately say, "Of course you don't understand me or know what happened to me. I don't understand myself and I'm not sure what happened to me, either!"

At this point, I want to focus on two provocative points made by Dr. Nijenhuis and other authors of the paper I cited previously called "Trauma-related Structural Dissociation of the Personality." First, they hit hard on the fact that the EP's memories are not, in a pure sense, factual. They may include some embellishment, omit certain elements, and/or have some degree of fantasy or misperception mixed in. As a corollary, the authors note that "another distinctive feature of traumatic memories is that upon their reactivation, access to many other memories is more or less obstructed."[2] In other words, the EP makes sure that the person's ability to deliver the facts, especially as they fit into the context of the person's life, is diminished even further.

Second, regarding Myers's work on EP and ANP and the emergence of the term multiple personality disorder, the authors say,

> One may object to labeling structurally dissociated mental systems as "personalities." In fact, for this reason, the DSM-IV converted the label "multiple personality disorder" into "dissociative identity disorder." Nevertheless, it is important to appreciate that both ANP and EP display "enduring patterns of perceiving, relating to, and thinking about the environment and [them]selves."[3]

What we've come to know, then, is that the different personalities of someone with DID will have shared memories, as I noted in chapter 5, but the way they recall those memories will be different. In consonance with that, the way they behave will tend to be very different. Another way of considering the dissociative phenomenon is that parallel states of consciousness exist in the brain.

In the final episode of the TV series *M*A*S*H*, Captain Hawkeye Pierce finds himself in a mental hospital trying to deal with post-trauma problems that are immobilizing him. The psychiatrist, Dr. Sidney Freedman, tries to help him recall certain events, which Hawkeye remembers incorrectly. The most poignant is his memory of being on a bus filled with South Korean refugees and wounded soldiers on their way to the MASH (Mobile Army Surgical Hospital) unit for treatment. Their journey takes them into close proximity to an enemy patrol; the bus pulls over and everyone must be absolutely silent or jeopardize their lives. Hawkeye remembered that there had been a Korean woman holding a squawking chicken and he told her to shut the damn thing up. The sound stopped. During his therapy, the truth emerged: There was no chicken. Hawkeye remembered that the woman had killed a bird because he could not handle the reality that she had suffocated her own baby to save the lives of everyone else.

Going back to the lay person and the desire for facts, what is a spouse or friend who does not have trauma-induced dissociation supposed to do in the face of conflicting stories, strange behavior, and sudden recollections of horrible things that were never mentioned in all the years they have known the person?

When you look at the person dearest to you—the *one* you love—you want to see consistency. Erratic behavior, uncharacteristically critical remarks, and other bad surprises make you want the *one* you love to return to normal. In the yearning for consistency, we try to make sense of the aberrations. Excuses abound: "She's just in a bad mood." "He must have had a terrible day at the office." "She always gets like this after her mother calls."

This is what people around Saroj Parida did. They searched endlessly for explanations that would make his behavior understandable and logical, so their beloved colleague, friend, husband, father could be the *one* they cared about.

He did have oneness in terms of a persistent and pervasive care for the well-being of babies, a personal and professional priority that earned him the nickname "The Infant Whisperer."[4] Long before his DID diagnosis, and the ability to name alters that included Baby and five-year-old Sissy, he told the journalist who gave him the nickname that he always prefers the kids' table at parties. "I think my brain stopped growing when I was four years old," he told her. "I can relate better to kids than adults." When Maryann visited him at Otisville Federal Correctional Institution, it was a sunny August afternoon and a number of the other inmates' families filled the outdoor visiting area. Several young children found a reason to interact with Saroj; one of the little ones kept tossing a ball in his direction. A toddler decided to come up and simply introduce herself by clinging to his leg. More than adults, children around Saroj pick up his "oneness." This trait was evident in him even when he was a child himself. When Saroj entered medical school, it was a foregone conclusion for most people close to him that his strong love for children would lead him to the specialty of treating infants and children. All of this has reinforced my hypothesis that the "oneness" in Saroj's life stopped at around age four or five, coinciding with the onset of his abuse, after which his personality fragmented.

The challenge for Saroj is to find his oneness as an adult: to merge the different versions of "the truth" and come up with a coherent personality with a coherent memory that gives the consciously remembered traumatic events a place in his life without destroying it.

SELF-MEDICATING

After Robert's diagnosis of bipolar disorder, he chose to seek help from a practitioner of homeopathic medicine. At first, his wife Emily supported his efforts to stay away from pharmaceuticals and pursue a path of "natural" maintenance, since they were both smart enough to realize that homeopathy did not promise healing, but rather a way of subduing symptoms. That got old fast. The dozen vials involving three-drops-of-this four times a day and two-drops-of-that once a day became too complicated and made an ordinary weekend trip a scheduling nightmare. He went back to the psychiatrist who made the diagnosis and Robert committed to taking the prescribed medications—until that, too, became a burden. Taking the "meds" meant that he could not consume alcohol. After a few months of trying to adapt, he gave up and self-medicated. Emily and Robert's next-door neighbor just happened to have a business that was helping to put him through law school: He sold marijuana. Behind Emily's back, Robert became a good customer of the neighbor's and that is when the most severe behavioral problems emerged. Robert felt fine—perhaps better than he had in a long time—and that meant that he went into complete denial about having a mental illness. He concluded that his psychiatrist was wrong. His wife was wrong. His symptoms were "gone," so they must be the ones with the problem.

He took off on another road trip, but this time, it wasn't an instructor from skydiving facility that called her: It was the police. They had stopped him for speeding and spotted a bag of pot sitting openly on the car seat next to him. Thanks to insightful officers, Robert made another trip to the psychiatric ward instead of jail.

Renowned interventionist and bestselling author, Ken Seeley, makes a point with which I agree completely: "There is a great preponderance of addiction amongst the mentally ill."[5] As a corollary, with self-medicating being a significant problem among people with mental disorders, they may find themselves seeking help for the addiction, mistakenly thinking that it's causing all of the other unstable behaviors. They can go years, or maybe all their lives, not realizing that there is another problem comingled with the addiction: mental illness.

DEATH BY DEFERENCE

With some help, but not necessarily the right kind, people who suffer from dissociative disorders can seem to pull themselves together. In fact, they might have a professional and/or social network that demands that they act normal.

Our society has put a revolving-door phenomenon in place. We want our loved ones—as well as society's geniuses and stars—back doing what they are "supposed to do," no matter what the cost to them or to ourselves. They have to try to act normal to support a family, raise the kids, and entertain us.

Saroj Parida had many people around him "protecting" him from discovering the severity of his problem. There is the relatively benign assistance his wife would give him at a party by reminding him the names of people he had met over and over, but didn't recall because people with DID have extended memory lapses. On the other end of the spectrum were the colleagues who made excuses for his bizarre behavior and covered up for him when he did something odd. That was their way of treating his symptoms. And then there were the insurance companies he bilked.

I'd venture to say that a great many people reading this book have, at least at some point, filed an insurance claim that was rejected. Most of us share the opinion that insurance companies do more than conduct due diligence on claims; they seek reasons to reject claims. But Saroj Parida, with an alter at the helm, billed insurance companies for services that not only weren't performed for infants, but couldn't possibly have been performed for them because they weren't born yet or they were a different gender, or any number of ridiculously obvious reasons. He collected about 7 million dollars in fraudulent claims by the time the FBI showed up at his door. In the two years he perpetrated these activities, insurance companies would occasionally reject a claim or ask for their money back. Saroj, as himself, would wonder how such a mistake happened and simply write a check to the insurance company to cover the "error." By not manifesting some curiosity about the odd claims for many months, and simply accepting the returned funds as admission of an innocent mistake, the insurance companies ironically may have inadvertently, implicitly also "made excuses" for Saroj's symptoms.[6]

And there are countless examples of people like the veterans studied by Dr. Spiegel, who never got better because medical professionals treated only their symptoms in an effort to help them appear normal.

USE AND MISUSE OF COGNITIVE-BEHAVIORAL THERAPY

The National Association of Cognitive-Behavior Therapists defines Cognitive-Behavioral Therapy (CBT) as follows:

> Cognitive-Behavioral Therapy is a form of psychotherapy that emphasizes the important role of thinking in how we feel and what we do. . . . CBT is based on the Cognitive Model of Emotional Response. Cognitive-behavioral therapy is based on the idea that our *thoughts* cause our feelings and behaviors, not external things, like people, situations, and events. The benefit of this fact is that we can change the way we think to feel/act better even if the situation does not change.[7]

Why make a special point of discussing CBT in a chapter addressing the hazards of treating the symptoms? First, let me assure you that I have no vendetta with CBT or its practitioners. In fact, I frequently use the fundamental principles of CBT in my psychotherapeutic treatment of many of my patients. The British used to whimsically refer to psychiatrists as the "brain police." Indeed, I believe we all would do well to maintain the habit of routinely "policing" our thoughts and attitudes, for undeniably what we think can affect how we feel and behave, for better or worse. But however helpful this brain policing might be at times, at other times it is simply not sufficient, for a few reasons.

First, there is ample evidence in neurological and psychiatric research that cognition (thinking) in the absence of emotional input is ineffective at best. In his book *Descartes' Error*,[8] Antonio Damásio illustrates this point in the example of Phineas Gage, to whom I referred in chapter 3. As I noted, as a result of a railroad construction accident, Gage lost his ability to generate the emotions necessary to help him make moral and socially acceptable decisions. In essence, the injury severed the connections between the "emotional" and "cognitive" portions of Gage's brain. Neurologist Damásio explains how this makes René Descartes ("I think, therefore I am.") wrong in proffering the idea that the human mind is separate from bodily processes.

Now let's for a moment learn a lesson from even further back in time, through this story told by my late, wonderful friend Leo Madow, MD, in his book *Love: How to Understand and Enjoy It.* King Frederick of Sicily devised an experiment to discover what language children would speak spontaneously if they never heard language. So he ordered foster mothers to take excellent care as usual of newborn babies, except that they were not to utter any sounds while caring for them, including cooing. What language did they ultimately speak? None, because these well-fed, well-bathed babies all died![9] They died from lack of emotional input. And indeed, modern research provides ever-more evidence of the importance of early (even prenatal) emotional input from outside for adequate cognitive development in the human being.

Secondly, while we originally learn how and what to think in relationship with our mothers (and fathers), in normal healthy development throughout the life cycle we never lose nor outgrow the importance of emotional input from other persons in clarifying and sometimes in altering what we think. In essence, autism is a condition wherein the individual is inaccessible to the emotional input of other persons. Non-autistic persons who lose or avoid the potential influence of others often begin to seem a bit autistic.

For these reasons alone, adequate psychotherapeutic healing for persons with mental illness secondary to trauma must take into consideration the relationship factors present when the trauma occurred and, just as importantly, the relationship factors in the healing process—that is, in the relationship between the therapist and the patient. Given this reality, the following becomes evident:

- The most effective treatment approaches for post-traumatic and dissociative disorders are those informed by theories that incorporate relationship factors into the treatment (such as psychodynamic and relational theories).
- The most effective CBT practitioners in applying their methodology to treatment of post-traumatic and dissociative disorders are those who exude particular empathic warmth in their interaction with the patient, and thereby inject necessary emotional input into their cognitive-behavioral approach. Unfortunately, sometimes psychotherapists are attracted to CBT out of discomfort with their own emotions, if not those of others. This severely restricts their ability to be helpful to

patients, especially when the treatment is more prolonged and complicated as it is with most victims of repeated trauma.

With these qualifiers in mind, you might wonder why CBT has gained such ascendency in modern psychotherapy. Firstly, CBT is far easier to "manualize" than the more relationally oriented psychotherapies like psychodynamic psychotherapy. That is, CBT can be more easily taught and applied in training centers. The relationship-focused therapies are far more difficult to teach and learn, typically requiring years of didactic instruction and individual supervision in order to develop the skills necessary to be truly proficient. And then there's the unavoidable reality that there is a certain artistry to being a good relationship-based therapist that, somewhat like the skills of a good athlete, musician, or actor, cannot be taught. So the temperamental and personality variables requisite to be a good relational therapist are harder to identify and find.

I am always reminded in this discussion of the principles of sound psychotherapy advocated by my good friend and outstanding teacher Dr. Daniel Hughes, whose Dyadic Developmental Psychotherapy technique[10] is gaining worldwide ascendency as a preferred treatment for children with attachment and post-traumatic stress disorders. Dan uses the acronym PACE, which I firmly believe can be used as a set of principles in all psychotherapeutic settings with adults as well as with children. The "P" is playfulness: the therapist must somehow impart a certain lightheartedness that reminds the patient that there is brightness to this world that they can glimpse even in the midst of their pain. The "A" is for unconditional acceptance of the patient, while not necessarily of his or her behavior or beliefs. The "C" is for curiosity, the open-mindedness on the part of the therapist regarding the meaning of the patient's behavior that prevents quick, gratuitous, and often simply erroneous conclusions and treatments, as noted above. And the "E" is for empathy, that all-important striving to understand the patient's emotional state of mind for what it is, rather than as a projection of one's own agenda or state of mind.

While therapeutic approaches such as Dan's and other relationship-based approaches do not currently have the research "evidence base" as does CBT, on the other hand they are rich in "practice-based evidence"—that is, countless case examples of persons successfully treated. Unfortunately, in our current medical-economic climate, for various reasons case studies are routinely dismissed as scientifically soft and unreliable. At worst, this state of affairs can actually lead to the error of dismissing the validity of the diagnosis of DID merely for lack of an "evidence-based" treatment for it. I will explore this, and an expanded view of PACE, in the subsequent chapters.

Christa's mom failed to be curious about her child's behavior when Christa ran around the room screeching and flapping her cape. Her failure of curiosity led to a failure of empathy. Based on the severity of the punishment that ensued, it's clear that Christa and her alter Judge did not feel unconditionally accepted—something that also couldn't occur without curiosity on the part of the parents. For a person who is dissociation-prone, the lack of those principles in action creates a spawning ground for dissociation. And when the therapist fails to apply them, the dissociative disorder can get worse rather than better. It's vital to remain deeply curious about a person's symptoms because it's that curiosity that empowers all of us involved with the person—clinicians or loved ones—to be genuinely helpful.

WHAT SYMPTOMS TELL US

As we prepare to enter a robust discussion of treatment and healing, consider the case of Sally, whose symptoms, personality, and responses came together to make it clear to me what kind of therapies she needed.

Sally was a fifty-eight-year-old woman in treatment for several years for complex post-traumatic stress disorder. Early and repeated emotional trauma had left enduring scars in her personality, distorting the manner in which she perceives others and thereby thinks and feels about them, and ultimately how she interacts with them. At one point in her treatment Sally painfully shared that her parents admitted that she was "supposed to be a boy," and they were extremely disappointed when she emerged female. Her childhood memories bore witness that they never overcame their disappointment, as they habitually responded to her normal occasional childhood misbehavior and shortcomings with disgust and excessive punishment.

Because of the early and repeated assaults to her self-image, Sally was left in adult life with extreme insecurity in her attachments to significant others in her life. This insecurity was to the extent that she would misperceive others as rejecting of her, and then either withdraw from them or retaliate accusatorily against them. In other words, Sally was endlessly repeating in her here-and-now relationships the original scenario of her life, wherein as an infant and toddler she routinely experienced her world as uninterested in if not actively rejecting of her. When she inevitably re-enacted this same scenario in her relationship with me, we had an opportunity to do some healing work.

Upon greeting Sally in the waiting room, I could immediately sense Sally's state of mind by her response. That is, if she'd had a difficult week at work or with family or friends she would perceive me as frustrated that I had to meet with her, and she would wear a countenance connoting a mixture of wariness and anger. This would sometimes result in an accusation that I'd seemed in recent weeks to have become cold and "clinical." Earlier in the course of her treatment, Sally would sometimes apologize for taking up my time, or at other times storm toward the office door threatening to leave and drive her car into a tree. Over the course of her treatment, Sally ultimately accepted and embraced my interpretation that she was re-enacting in her relationship with me the early scenes in her life, in which the hard-wired circuit in her brain was activated to say, "The one on whom I'm utterly dependent wants nothing to do with me, because I'm no good, he/she is no good, or we're both no good." Eventually Sally's chronic and recurrent episodes of acute anxiety and depression remitted, and the quality of her relationships improved substantially.

What were the necessary ingredients of the talk therapy for Sally—and why did I rule out certain therapies, concluding that they might treat the symptoms, but not the cause?

The single most important ingredient was the establishment of a strong therapeutic alliance between Sally and me, one in which both of us felt that we were sitting on a fence looking out over the pasture of her life experiences, and together putting together a story of her life (technically called "co-construction of narrative") that made sense of her current struggles in relationships as a natural consequence of her earlier ones.

Quite regularly would I call to Sally's attention her negatively distorted thinking ("Dr. Biever is glad I'm going on vacation, so he doesn't have to see me for a week," or "My daughter isn't visiting because I didn't raise her right"), reminding her in so many words that she needed to be a good "brain policeman" for herself. In the later stage of treatment Sally steadily became better at catching herself falling back into old negative thinking patterns, and replacing them with more positive, more realistic ones.

However, to understand the relentless persistence of these distorted thoughts, we had to understand the *misperceptions* that underpinned them: at those moments Sally was convinced that she picked up something in my behavior that signified that I couldn't stand her. In turn, we were able to relate these habitual misperceptions to the infantile state of affairs wherein she got millions of unfortunately accurate messages from her parents that she was a disappointment to them, hard-wiring a very sad belief in her self-image circuitry.

As necessary as this new understanding was, it wasn't sufficient for Sally, and usually is not sufficient for countless others who have suffered such repeated damage to their perceptions of self and others via early childhood neglect, and/or physical or emotional abuse. Instead, Sally's recovery required direct here-and-now experiences of being respected, valued, and admired by me as her therapist. That is, it wouldn't be sufficient for me to point out to her that her husband, children, or boss respected, valued, and admired her. For those confrontations to be credible, she had to feel it directly from me. In more technical terms, Sally had to undergo a *corrective emotional experience* in her therapy by way of confrontation time and time again with the reality that I truly did (and do) respect, value, and admire her.

So how does this corrective emotional experience happen? Here's where the cutting edge of the sophisticated psychotherapeutic system called *relational psychodynamic psychotherapy*—which is built on psychoanalytic principles—gives seasoned therapists additional insight in helping these deeply wounded patients. Namely, it carefully delineates those circumstances wherein the therapist's own feelings about the patient can safely and necessarily be brought into the therapy. For example, at times I would say to Sally some variant of, "You know, you just truly amaze me, how you find a way to be so kind to your mother now when she hurt you so often as a little girl!" Or, "It saddens me to know that you thought I'd rather not see you at the supermarket, because it really was fun to get to talk with you there." Or, "I must tell you, I'm feeling angry now that you're once again accusing me of looking down on you as a second-class citizen, when I can't find any evidence of that attitude either in myself or in how I've ever treated you." (Now, as necessary as such confrontations as the latter one are for a more complete corrective emotional experience, they may initially evoke shame in the patient. So I would always be prepared to relate Sally's misperception right back to the early, deeply worn groove in her psyche over which she had no control as an infant and toddler.)

Finally, I was constantly mindful of the importance of keeping the therapeutic experience "light" enough for Sally so that therapy itself would not be a repetition of her early trauma. She found it very comforting to be offered a cup of coffee at the beginning of the therapy hour. And she enjoyed being kidded about her penchant for clever accessorizing with items found in a local thrift shop. I also enjoyed making sport of myself at times when I'd made a mistake, which she found delightful and no doubt became part of her corrective emotional experience ("If this guy I respect so much doesn't take himself too seriously, I guess I don't have to either.")

You will note that I didn't refer to dissociation in this brief presentation of Sally's case. In fact, we did need to confront the emergence of the Isakower phenomenon rather early on in her treatment, that is, her perception that she physically moved alternately farther away and closer. But otherwise, she did not show any dissociative symptoms. Why? Sally falls solidly into the Apollonian personality type, and so it is no surprise that she would experience a minimum of dissociative symptoms.

Sally's case illustrates both the value and the limitations of Cognitive-Behavioral Therapy in treating persons with severe trauma-related psychiatric problems, be they dissociative or otherwise in symptom presentation. Each element of PACE is also evident in the description of the case; the role of each element comes to life even more in chapter 7. Finally, I hope that you are impressed with the importance of the full humanity of the therapist being very carefully brought into the treatment without violating the boundaries of therapy—a subject area we will now explore with even more vigor.

· 7 ·

Treatment That Heals

𝒯rauma triggers the adaptive mechanism of dissociation in trance-prone individuals. The therapist's deep empathic attunement to the plight of the dissociated person is essential for healing. Empathy imparts genuine caring and respect; it doesn't accuse or lay blame. But the empathic approach, however necessary, is not sufficient. Enough time with the patient is necessary in order to establish the trusting "therapeutic alliance" between therapist and patient that will enable the patient to allow his dissociative defenses to gradually melt away. For that reason, you will not find anything in this chapter that advocates short "efficient" sessions in treating someone with a dissociative disorder. The infamous "fifteen-minute medication check" into which most of our modern psychiatrists and their patients are shoehorned is unfortunately an example of almost routinely inadequate time to understand and effectively treat the patient. The following story is far from an isolated example.

I once supervised psychiatry residents in a medication clinic for children at Penn State University's Hershey Medical Center. One day a nine-year-old boy came in for his periodic medication check. He'd had a couple of good years on Ritalin, but during this visit his grandmother announced that he needed a change. He had recently begun to complain of a crawling sensation on the skin of his arms and hands. She had done her homework and read that Ritalin can cause such a sensation (technically referred to as "formication," from the Latin word for "ant").

In a standard, fifteen-minute medication check—which gives the psychiatrist about eight minutes of actual working time with the patient—he would have had almost no time to entertain other possible explanations. Consequently, regardless of the child's relatively long history of responding well to the current medication, the psychiatrist would probably prescribe an alternate drug, thus setting in motion a possible miserable cycle of "try this, try that" until the child responds well again.

In this clinic, I kept the medication visits to half-hour intervals, for the sake of adequate assessment and decision making while simultaneously teaching the resident. In this instance as in so very many, the half hour was necessary in order to understand what was really going on.

By way of background, the grandmother had been estranged from the boy's mother for a number of years. One midsummer afternoon, the grandmother and a friend of hers were shopping and saw a little boy crawling atop a dumpster looking for food. Flies covered his arms and hands. The grandmother said, "Isn't that pathetic! Look at that child." Her friend responded, "That's your grandson." The estrangement had occurred before the birth of the little boy, and so although her friend knew of the boy's identity, the grandmother did not. Immediately, the grandmother took action to get legal custody of the boy.

Fast-forward to the medication check. I asked the grandmother to fill us in about the boy's current circumstances. We learned that on a recent morning, just before the formications began, there was a knock at the door and the little boy answered it. It was his mother. He hadn't seen her since the day he'd been rescued from the dumpster. He registered shock and extreme fear.

The grandmother accepted my interpretation that there may be a correlation between seeing the mother—threatening to come back into his life again—and getting the feeling that bugs were crawling on his skin. He was simply experiencing a traumatic memory. We agreed to continue the Ritalin and see what happened since the grandmother had no intention of letting her daughter play a role in her child's life anytime soon. As the boy became certain of his safety, the crawling sensation soon went away.

I often use this example to illustrate "penny wise and pound foolish" to residents and colleagues whom "the system" is steering away from talk therapy, which is the general term I'm going to apply to the kind of therapy that's necessary with patients who have dissociative disorders.

THE WHO AND WHAT OF TREATMENT

Psychotherapy is the umbrella term for the scores of named "talk therapy" approaches to helping person suffering from a mental illness. Although each school of psychotherapy—psychodynamic psychotherapy, cognitive-behavioral therapy, and so on—has distinctive core features, different practitioners show considerable variability in technique and style, affected by such individual features as the personality, training, and experience of the therapist. A detailed review of the various most commonly practiced schools of psychotherapy and their approach to dissociative disorders is well beyond the scope of this book. Instead, I will focus on psychodynamic psychotherapy, the approach that I utilize as my theoretical foundation for understanding and treating my patients.

The original and by far the most intensive form of psychodynamic psychotherapy is psychoanalysis, developed by Sigmund Freud a century ago and evolved greatly in theory and technique even up to the present. Psychoanalysis is a three-to-five session per week therapy for however many years it takes to complete the process. Psychoanalytic psychotherapy is an approach based on psychoanalytic principles, but typically involves sessions at far less frequent intervals and for shorter periods of time. While psychoanalysis often continues to position the patient "on the couch," psychoanalytic psychotherapy is usually conducted face to face.

Psychoanalysis is provided only by trained analysts who have taken several years of focused coursework, personally undergone analysis, and then performed successful analyses under supervision. (There are qualified "lay analysts," by the way, meaning they do not hold a medical degree.) This process of analysis goes into greater depth than psychoanalytic psychotherapy. Because of the intensity of the experience, the patient capable of undergoing an analysis will explore in great depth his conscious and unconscious memories of early life experiences, fantasies, dreams, and even bodily sensations and functions, and their role in creating and maintaining current problems in living. Psychoanalysis is more costly in time and money than other psychotherapies, and is not necessary for adequate treatment of most mental illnesses. Nevertheless, we all should feel deeply indebted to those who practice and undergo psychoanalysis. Why? Although psychoanalysis has been the butt of good-natured—and at times not-so-good-natured—humor in the media and on screen over the years, and while there is variability in the quality of analysts just as in any other profession, this field continues to make remarkable contributions to our ever-greater understanding of the intricate workings of the human mind and how we can better help in its healing through relationship. In fact, in this day and age of radically restricted insurance funding for psychotherapy, psychoanalysis is as much a research tool as it is an applied therapeutic modality. Dr. Martha Stark's work exemplifies this. She is an adult and child psychiatrist/psychoanalyst who has written three award-winning books on psychoanalytic theory and technique. A lot of her insights regarding *relational psychotherapy* and *relational psychoanalysis*, which have an emphasis on the role of both real and imagined relationships in mental illness and healing, arose out of her psychoanalytic work.[1] I have a concern, in fact, that there is an erosion of opportunity for young psychiatrists to become analysts because of the pressure to stick to constricting timetables and produce quick results.

I don't want you to get bogged down in technical detail. So now that I've drawn a distinction between psychoanalysis and other psychotherapies, I just want to emphasize three points before I switch to using one simple term primarily: talk therapy.

The first is a cautionary note that builds on something noted DID specialist Richard Kluft, MD, expressed in his book, *Clinical Perspectives on Multiple Personality Disorder*. Kluft's argument that some therapists "force MPD patients to conform to their preferred theories and practices" (a circumstance he labeled "Procrustean rigidity")[2] is not only something with which I wholeheartedly agree, but a practice I wholeheartedly abhor, whether the person has multiple personalities or any other mental illness. Regardless of what the clinician calls the therapy—cognitive-behavioral, psychodynamic, or anything else—if the therapist is unwilling or unable to accommodate his theoretical orientation and/or clinical approach well enough to "meet the patient where he's at," the treatment will simply not work. After a careful discussion of the treatment concerns with the therapist, the patient may need to look elsewhere for help. Otherwise stated, our *belief* that our doctors can help us is an indispensable ingredient in our recovery. But so is our doctor's ability to connect well enough with us with understandings and skills adequate to bring about progress. In short, don't get overly attached to a name, or "brand" of therapy, but rather focus on its effectiveness.

The next two points are about the nature of psychotherapy that I (and colleagues) see as necessary for a patient who has a dissociative disorder. First, it needs to be an in-depth approach, allowing for adequate time for patient and therapist to discover the story behind the dissociative symptoms and to find a way beyond them. Secondly, the therapy involves a relationship between the patient and the clinician, and in the case of DID, a relationship with the alters that together compose the cognitive and emotional makeup of the dissociating person.

Examples of two specific therapeutic actions that commonly occur in talk therapy were referenced briefly in the story of Sally in chapter 6: corrective emotional experience and co-construction of narrative. Saroj could dissociate into an alter if he perceived that the person with whom he was interacting would not accept his own emotional state and would either retaliate or withdraw from him. Therefore, my unwavering unconditional acceptance of him and all of his alters would be necessary if he were to feel it safe to "own" all of the feelings his mind had shunted off into alters over the years: in other words, to have a corrective emotional experience in the treatment that would lead to his ability to stay within his core self in other emotionally charged social situations.

A key aim of co-constructing the narrative of a traumatic past with a patient is to detoxify the memory of trauma that provoked dissociation. One of the things I do to detoxify the memory is to express not only my empathy—that's a given; they count on me to be sensitive to their plight in the midst of the trauma—but also to express my admiration sincerely for their mind's resourcefulness and resilience. "How did you survive that?" I ask. "The power of your little child's mind to endure that—and here you sit now!" (In truth, it does amaze me!) With that, they can look back on their situation and see it as something other than a sad story of ignorance and helplessness. It wouldn't help to say, "It wasn't your fault. There's nothing you could have done about it." At best that approach would relieve the burden of guilt by adding an even greater burden of the shame of helplessness. In reality, there *is* something they did about it: their amazing minds adapted and helped them move on and grow up. It's more accurate to say, "Wow! You survived that."

That is a key part of co-construction of narrative. In doing this, therapists are not gilding the lily for the benefit of the patient, but rather helping them understand and feel the story in a different way. We are telling a story realistically, simply emphasizing the positive part—that is, the survivor is amazing. For example, I would cite here the adaptive power of Saroj's mind to sequester into various alters emotions that could have killed him. The serious mischief done by some of them realistically spared Saroj and others of far more dire long-term consequences. This discovery in the course of our co-constructed narrative then facilitated Saroj's corrective emotional experience, helping him to accept in his core self the responsibility for the conduct of his mischievous alters and thereby relieving himself of the need for them.

It's important to maintain a distinction between talk therapy and what we might call an "encounter" with a clinician, because not every session a patient has with a psychiatrist or psychologist is necessarily a therapeutic one. One example of that in Saroj's case was the interview he had with the prosecution's psychiatrist, who was hired to "evaluate" him. The psychiatrist properly made it clear at the outset that there was a specific purpose to that interview, and it was not to set the stage for ongoing therapy. And in consultation liaison psychiatry, in more cases than not the consulting psychiatrist is not going to go on to treat the person.

I pause to make a point of this because of my strong conviction that every mental health professional engaging in any type of clinical interaction with a patient should be purposeful about rendering that person afterward more comfortable in the presence of mental health professionals. And that includes forensic evaluations, custody evaluations, and any others that can so easily leave the person with an enduring impression of mental health professionals as prying and judgmental. If anything, this principle should be even more imbedded in the approach of psychiatrists charged with the seemingly adversarial task of evaluating for the prosecution or defense.

THE PROCESS AND PRACTICE OF TREATMENT FOR DISSOCIATIVE DISORDERS

Building on Richard Kluft's twelve "pragmatic principles for the treatment of MPD,"[3] I offer the following interpretation, more of a layman's version of excellent guidance to clinicians. I'm also relating them specifically to elements of both the formal therapy with Saroj Parida and the circumstantial therapeutic elements of his prison experience. The latter illustrates how the process of healing cannot just be an isolated experience confined to the sessions behind the heavy doors and on the comfortable couch of a therapist's office. This is a point continued and emphasized in chapter 8.

As you consider these treatment principles, keep in mind that they are not sequential steps, but instead concurrent in the treatment.

Keep Clear and Consistent Boundaries

Dr. Kluft's discussion of broken interpersonal boundaries being at the root of the patient's problem constitutes a reminder to therapists to stay focused on the therapy and not inadvertently repeat boundary violations in the therapy relationship. Having had the experience of a patient with the unusual condition of DID in one of the most extraordinary intellects I have ever encountered—namely, Saroj Parida—I have experienced how easy it would be for a therapist to get caught up in the uniqueness of the situation, contemplate writing a paper or a book, give lectures rife with dramatic detail of alters emerging . . . and lose track of therapy. Kluft warns of this very thing, so this particular pragmatic principle clearly aims at keeping the therapist focused on the patient instead of his own personal interests, goals, and self-aggrandizing exercises.

As is typical for Odysseans like me, I tend to have a rhythmic vacillation between action and reflection. If either tendency were to get too strong a hold on me in a case such as Saroj's, I would be in danger of violating Kluft's first principle. For example, after each session with Saroj I would take the usual action of writing a "progress note." Reflecting on the session, I'd want to include all the richness of the session in my note—which would take forever. To complicate matters, I'd be mindful that recording all of that detail would be useful for a book—you're beginning to see where this could lead! That type of back-and-forth is a typical Odyssean dilemma. Of course, as it turns out my yearning for additional reflection has been satisfied nicely by hours of wonderful dialogue with my coauthor, to whom Saroj graciously allowed me to tender his treatment records. More routinely it was satisfied by my presentation of Saroj's case frequently at the weekly supervision meetings held by my colleagues and me, wherein not only do we offer several different sets of "eyes and ears" on difficult cases but also keep each other oriented to potential boundary problems in our therapeutic relationships. (If I haven't previously impressed my professional brothers and sisters as to the importance of regular supervision, let me do it now.)

There is another perspective on the issue of boundaries, however, this one shared with us by Saroj himself. He noted that prison inmates in general have an extraordinary need to both maintain their own boundaries and to respect other's. He is finding remarkable consistency in the way his cohorts interrelate with him, and feels that this in itself is not an insignificant part of his healing process. He recently noted in an email to me,

> Having boundaries (as you told me Dr. Kluft described them) is a point well taken. Not having been fully aware of this concept going into prison makes it even more relevant and significant in my case since I experienced the importance firsthand before I knew it theoretically. Boundaries are pretty well defined by the BOP [Bureau of Prisons] and the fear factor associated with transgressing them has definitely helped in my healing.

Boost the Perception of Mastery and Control

DID patients have chunks of time missing and may have people telling them about odd behaviors that seem incredibly inconsistent with their "normal" way of acting. As a result, they can easily feel out of control and helpless. They need to understand how they are active, intelligent participants in their treatment. As a fellow physician, Saroj had an exceptionally high interest in the literature related to his condition and he borrowed books, researched journal articles, and committed with both his heart and his head to achieving mastery so he could help me help him. He continues that reading and research in prison and, in fact, gave us an initial round of edits on this manuscript.

In day-to-day prison activities, too—whether it was fellow inmates asking him to conduct an art class when they saw his random sketches, or getting him to coach them in ping pong when he won the camp tournament—Saroj has been able to regain a sense of mastery. After years of recognition as a multitalented genius, his acceptance that he was a person with a serious mental illness who had committed crimes had eroded his sense of self-esteem.

Establish and Maintain a Strong Therapeutic Alliance

In a journal article, Maryann once documented a project involving diagnostic decision trees developed by some of the doctors in the telemedicine team at Walter Reed Army Medical Center. One of the aims of the article was to help doctors who had to function outside of their specialty while in the battlefield. For example, if a soldier seeing an ophthalmologist had a facial rash that suggested the possibility of lupus, he might be able to use a dermatology logic tree to rule it out as a diagnosis or to reinforce his provisional diagnosis.

If the problem is a rash, a doctor can certainly use a decision tree upfront. But an algorithm like that has no place in any early interaction if the problem is in the human mind. The first step can never be pulling out a decision tree to progress analytically through symptoms.

The first and most important focus of a psychiatric session must be the establishment of a strong therapeutic alliance. It's the *sine qua non*: If that doesn't happen, then nothing good will come of the attempts at treatment. Looking at the case of Saroj, I needed to make him feel comfortable and trusting enough to be able to come back a second time. Our therapy would not have stood a chance of becoming an ongoing, successful relationship without an emotional "handshake."

Our first meeting occurred on March 6, 2009—he was anxious and tentative, often kneeling or sitting on the floor as he spoke, and sometimes standing up to make a point—with a follow-up phone call that afternoon.

By the time we met the next morning, he was relatively calm with me. I got the feeling that we were going to be able to work together. This time, he didn't pace or kneel on the floor. He stayed in his seat and started opening up about deeply personal aspects of his life, such as his religion and his children. And then he came forth with one of my favorite positive prognostic signs: humor! As he recalled occasionally thinking of the possibility of very tiny creatures somewhere in the universe, more intelligent than humans, we both noticed a bug crawling on the wall and laughed heartily.

The therapeutic alliance had begun to form.

Address Buried Trauma and the Emotions It Evokes

When Saroj was ready to share with me some detail regarding his childhood trauma, I was more interested in his affect than in discovering the literal blow-by-blow of what happened. By affect, I mean the demonstration of an emotion or set of emotions the memory evokes, such as a combination of anger and helplessness. In telling Saroj's story to friends in various settings, Maryann occasionally found people asking, "Did Dr. Biever validate that Saroj was sexually abused as a child?" She would help them to understand that the answer is quite irrelevant to the treatment, regardless of the evidence that he was. Paradoxical as it may seem, what actually happened has far less relevance to healing than what the memory arouses emotionally in the person.

I also can't assume there will be complete consistency among the stories, even though the stories of abuse do share certain key elements. As I've stated in several sections already, memory is contextual. Not only does the current context affect what a person remembers and how it's remembered, but circumstances surrounding the creation of the memory also make a big difference. In striving for a greater understanding of a patient's buried trauma, I hope to hear more of the patient's story—what happened just before that? Just after it? The next day?

A tornado that came through a town within two miles of my office leveled many homes before finally exhausting itself just beyond a local golf course. I remember thinking, "Why is the train noise coming from the south? It should be coming from the north." The "train" was the tornado.

My partner and I volunteered to talk with parents in the aftermath to fill them in on how their children were likely to react to the destruction and violence associated with the tornado. We found that these parents especially appreciated the concept of co-construction of narrative. They could then sit down with their children and reflect back on the tornado experience in a way that validated the full range of feelings they all—including the parents—had during and after the event, thereby minimizing any useless guilt or shame about their reactions to the trauma and the post-traumatic stress residue that could ensue from those unresolved feelings. Co-construction of narrative can also happen in advance of a trauma. For example, a sense of camaraderie and the way soldiers might grasp their situation and probable fate can mitigate the effects of a battle. Some of the World War II veterans interviewed for the TV series *Band of Brothers* illustrated this eloquently. Their survival of the emotional trauma of the terrible combat to which they were subsequently exposed was facilitated by their acceptance ahead of time of the probability that they would not survive the war, that death was likely to be imminent.

Consider the flip side of these stories of preventing or softening a negative response to trauma. What if, in the aftermath of the tornado, parents took their kids to visit the site of devastation and let them conjure up images of people screaming and puppies being hurled into the air?

Saroj told me a story made more poignant because it occurred while he was in the midst of ongoing sexual abuse by the house boy:

> When I was ten or eleven, I had bought some rat poison and had locked myself in the bathroom with the intention of killing myself after having been chased around a block by my brother brandishing a metal rod and screaming, "I'll kill you."

Was Saroj responding to his brother's (probably idle) threat, or was this just "one more thing" reinforcing his growing sense of worthlessness and fear?

For a therapist, addressing buried trauma is never a simple matter of getting the supposed facts of a story. Part of the treatment may well involve an effort to detoxify the memory by offering them other possibilities for how the scenario might have played out. For example at a point in the therapy I might say, "If only you had had someone in your life you could have gone to—but how could you, with your mind of a little child? You couldn't possibly be an adult and a child at the same time and understand how that was going to affect you later on?" And perhaps, "Had somebody, maybe like myself, been there at the time—if you'd had someone like me to talk to at the time—how much different would it have been?"

Reduce Separateness and Conflict among Alters

The concept put forth by Richard Kluft that alters "dissolve in the solvent of empathy"[4] gets to the essence of what DID is all about in the first place. If the therapist can accept the affects, opinions, and attitudes of all the alters, then so eventually will the host. That unconditional acceptance is easier said than done.

To what extent might someone feel as though she doesn't want to integrate an alter because it would be like killing a part of herself? It is possible that she would essentially consider it an abortion of a personality?

Saroj now talks about his inner family with affection and recognizes that each has a role of emotional responsibility to him. And as far as Christa is concerned, Judge will always be there, and perhaps always should be there. Depending on the goal of the therapy, a topic discussed in the next chapter, a therapist might say, "It's going to be very hard to say goodbye to Judge."

Regardless of whether the goal of therapy is integration or some other state of mental health in which the alters no longer cause impairment, the host can and should develop empathic feelings about each of the alters. Respect for all parties involved is part of the healing process. The host should want to welcome the alter "home."

Aim for Consistency

Kluft notes that people who have multiple personalities are highly hypnotiz-able, which is consistent with my testing that validates the high trance capac-ity, or Dionysian profile, of someone like Saroj Parida. Highly suggestible persons need as much predictability and stability as can be achieved by the therapist and the trappings of therapy. Can you imagine how confusing it would be for someone with a collection of alters to also have a therapist who shifted moods, met in rooms with very different décor, and changed the time of the appointment at the last minute?

Fifty-four days after my first session with Saroj—with more than twenty sessions in that period as well as phone conversations—I was unavoidably detained for our meeting. This ten-minute delay (think about how many times you have waited more than ten minutes in a doctor's waiting room) was enough to send him into an altered state. I saw him pacing outside, smoking a cigarette. When I later found him absent from the waiting room, I went outside and found him lying on his side on the grass, fingers at his mouth, apparently asleep. He was startled when I called his name. He arose, seeming disoriented, slowly moving about with small steps, getting his bearings in a minute or so.

To some extent, the predictability of a prison schedule is part of what addresses Saroj's need for consistency. He doesn't wonder if he will eat or if his bed will be in the same place as it was the day before. He doesn't wonder if the people around him will be different. He doesn't wonder if the color of paint on the walls will change.

When he was moved from the facility in Otisville to the one in Lew-isburg, I saw this as a positive change to help him make the transition, ul-timately, to the outside world. Much of the regularity and predictability of the prison environment would remain, but some significant details would be different. His adjustment seems to support my hopeful hypothesis.

Treat All Personalities as "Created Equal"

The scenario that gave rise to a patient's DID involved someone acting out of character, doling out different and conflicting messages. It was a parent who nurtured some of the time, but abused some of the time. It was a teacher who cared and imparted knowledge some of the time, but psychologically or physically tortured the child the rest of the time. In short, inconsistency in relationships helped give rise to the problem, and so it is vital that the in-consistency not be repeated by treating one alter as "less than" and another as "more than." Each has a part. Each needs respect.

Part of what Saroj had to deal with—and this was confirmed by his brother who supposedly wanted to kill him with the metal rod—was a childhood filled with people who gave him sharply conflicting emotional messages. For example, the brother confirmed the "volcanic" temper of their father and the fact that it often took special aim at Saroj. This is the same father who praised Saroj for his genius and showed great pride at his accomplishments. The man who smashed dishes seemed like an even-tempered and calm individual publicly.

Restore Basic Assumptions

When Becky was a tiny child, her basic assumption was that mom loved her, her siblings loved her, and except for Dad's occasional outbursts, life was fine. Why did dad have occasional outbursts? She must have been a bad girl—that's what she concluded. As the abuse started and the negative experiences compounded, she held tight to the belief that she could ameliorate the situation by being a good girl.

I have seen with people like Saroj and Becky that it is not uncommon for them to punish themselves harshly as a result of feeling as though they somehow caused the problem. The therapist has a clear task: Help the patient move to an emotional place where the basic assumption is "This is not a normal situation. I didn't cause it and most people don't act that way."

Try to Avoid Overwhelming Experiences

A clinician treating a patient with DID would make a dramatic mistake by using implosion therapy. This is the kind of behavioral therapy sometimes used with phobia patients: You're afraid of heights, so I take you to the observation deck of the Space Needle in Seattle. Implosion therapy floods your consciousness with the thing you fear. It's important to pace the therapy for a dissociating patient because, as I said at the outset, the source of the disorder is trauma and depending on how the memory of that trauma is handled, it could become overwhelming.

Engender a Sense of Responsibility

One of the questions in the Structural Cluster Survey to which I referred in chapter 1 addresses the issue of responsibility. The question as phrased by the authors is as follows: "As you sense your responsibility for what you do, where do you place yourself on a scale of average, above or below?"[5] The person who responds "highly responsible" or "above average" gets an Apollonian rating for the question. The respondent who considers himself below average is more Dionysian, according to the authors. I maintain that this may be the weakest indicator in the survey, simply because so much of a person's sense of responsibility comes from cultural indoctrination, and in this case, "culture" could refer to family, religion, community, or even an organization like the Girl Scouts. Nonetheless, I defer to Drs. Herbert and David Spiegel, whose substantial body of research in trance capacity helped shape the survey.

With that question in mind, then, consider how the highly Dionysian person might express a natural tendency to look for external reasons why something went wrong. The possibility of the planets aligning in a particular way could be the cause of a pervasive sense of sadness or desperation in the world. An abundance of "negative energy" in the room could contribute to people leaving a party early. And who's to say that isn't the case? (The Apollonian reader is now saying, "Aw, c'mon!")

The challenge for a clinician treating a highly trance-prone person for DID then becomes pulling him more toward the center in terms of the responsibility rating. The process of engendering a heightened sense of personal responsibility through modeling, encouragement, and even overt urging sometimes needs to be part of the therapy.

The psychiatrist hired by the prosecution to evaluate Saroj did not agree with my diagnosis of DID—no surprise to me. In fact, I don't know that agreement with my diagnosis would have made any difference in the prosecution's assumption of Saroj's responsibility for his crimes—I would hope not!

From a clinical perspective, I saw very little choice other than for Saroj to take responsibility for what these alters did. First of all, legally, there is no precedent for using dissociative identity disorder successfully as a defense. But in a more fundamental way, I think there is something lost when someone wins a plea based on insanity. It can perpetuate a sense of personal powerlessness. Disavowal of responsibility becomes disavowal of personal power and integrity. So his acceptance of responsibility for what he did—albeit in these altered states—is part of the integrative process.

Other people's irresponsibility caused the problem in the first place, and in a way, we would perpetuate it by allowing the person to blame someone else—in this case, alternate personalities he was unaware of. An essential part of healing for the dissociating person is realizing that that other "person" who did the bad thing is actually himself.

Address and Correct Cognitive Errors

Dr. Kluft's advice here can just as easily apply to the therapist's communication with colleagues as with his patients. I have found with myself as well as with colleagues that the most common cognitive error regarding dissociation is forgetting that it commonly happens, and then failing to keep it in mind as a possible explanation for unusual patient behavior. Cognition—that is, thinking—can well be understood as a behavior in itself. And we humans are prone to behaving in ways inconsistent with what we believe or intend. So the therapist must foster in the patient a habit of constant vigilance of his thinking, so as to catch himself entertaining distorted, useless, or damaging thoughts.

As Saroj's case progressed, I received regular "supervision" from my colleagues here at our mental health center. Supervision in this context does not mean "do this, do that." Instead, it involves the sharing what happened in the therapy hour with fellow clinicians, followed by a frank discussion of what the patient shared (the "content") and how the therapist and patient dealt with the content (the "process"). Supervision gave me the benefit of other perspectives in the course of the treatment. In fact, I relied on supervision in Saroj's case to provide further scrutiny of my diagnostic impression of DID, resulting not only in my colleagues' support of the diagnosis but also their regular input regarding suggestions for treatment. Supervision should not be considered optional or "nice to have" for any mental health professional, no matter how seasoned and skilled. Nevertheless, many clinicians don't have the opportunity for supervision in their practices. It's considered a luxury and is not reimbursable. Many clinicians in inpatient and outpatient treatment systems feel compelled to pile up enough hours to justify their salary, and can't or don't want to take the time to have regularly scheduled meetings to discuss cases. I would go so far as to say that one excellent "quality of care" question for new patients seeking care is, "Do you have regular supervision?"

Show Humanity and Flexibility in Therapy

When patients with DID suffered the initial traumas that triggered dissociation, there were probably loving people around them who did nothing, either because they didn't know what was going on or because they were just passive players in the drama. Becky recalls that her mother took a relatively passive role in her life during the years of abuse, and didn't intervene until her father threatened to shoot everyone one night while he was in a drunken rage. Saroj recalls hiding under his mother's sari at times to escape his father's rage, but ultimately she did not protect him when his father decided to mete out physical punishment. And neither of the parents knew about the sexual abuse by the houseboy, so they couldn't stop that trauma.

For these reasons, it's essential that the therapist have an actively caring relationship with the patient. The therapist should also try to figure out what might be done to improve the patient's perception of being cared for by family and friends. Christa's therapist at Sierra Tucson, the in-patient psychiatric facility where she spent two months, invited her parents and her wife, Zoey, to have sessions as a family during the course of a week. Christa remembers it as a big step forward in her own self-acceptance and self-love, and the impetus for expressing genuine caring for the parents who had a role in her problems.

In my brief exchanges with inmates other than Saroj in the large room where prisoners all come together with their visitors, I sensed that they felt very warm toward him. And in both the Otisville and Lewisburg facilities, they seemed to rally around him, ask him for advice, and encourage him to teach art classes. In essence, many inmates added to the benefits of the structured environment by making it a positive and supportive environment as well. And, in small ways, they also protected him by letting him know when he did things that were not only a little "off," but against the prison rules. One example was alerting him when he inexplicably squirreled food away under his bed during an altered state—an offense that he knew to be potentially punishable by being put into isolation (known to inmates as "the hole").

Kluft's suggestion in this particular principle reminds me of the excellent teachings of my colleague, clinical child psychologist Dr. Dan Hughes. Dan is an expert in the treatment of attachment and post-traumatic stress disorders in children, and the author of such acclaimed books as *Attachment-Focused Parenting: Effective Strategies to Care for Children*. He originated the acronym PACE to capture the key elements of an effective therapeutic approach: playfulness, acceptance, curiosity, and empathy.

FOCUS ON PACE

Years ago at a psychoanalytic conference, a presenter cited some research on the question, "What are the active ingredients in psychotherapy?" The study concluded that of all the possible factors—seasoning of the therapist, theoretical orientation, time in treatment, and so on—the single most important ingredient was empathy.

With that concept of empathy as a starting point, Dan considers the other elements that seem vital in the treatment of our patients. His acronym PACE has appropriately evolved beyond an excellent psychotherapeutic mindset into a parenting philosophy. I am just as impressed with its applicability in the classroom and in daycare settings.

Playfulness

The word "play" itself has multiple synonymous that range from "fooling around" to the more toned-down "amusing yourself." In terms of therapy, probably the best way to think of play is as lightheartedness as opposed to undue gravity or solemnity. In treating any survivor of trauma, we are talking about terrible memories of horrible events in a person's life, but the element of playfulness helps to bring home the concept that there is much more to life than that trauma. When the therapist carefully uses playful moments in the course of treatment, the patient does not feel his problems minimized, but instead enjoys a glimpse into an equally real but joyful potential in his life.

Here we return for a moment to a prior discussion of the many different schools of psychotherapy. Some of them are naturally more amenable to blending in some playfulness. For example, in psychoanalytic therapies the so-called relational approach would more easily accommodate overt playfulness than the "classical" on-the-couch approach. Nevertheless, even in the latter instance, the analyst's playful tone of voice during "You know, I recall your having said you weren't going to go there anymore" might leave the patient feeling respected rather than scolded. Maybe it's like the popular demonstration with the jar first filled to the top with rocks, but then filled farther to the top with marbles, then with sand, but even then there's room for more, at which point the presenter pours in the beverage of choice with the punch line "There's always room for _____!" Whatever the type of therapy, there's always room for playfulness. In other words, playfulness can be an attitude.

It's important to note that being lighthearted about oneself can be very soothing or uplifting—perhaps the extreme example being the condemned man using "gallows humor" with his executioner. I have found that many times my not taking myself too seriously has rendered my patients able to ease off on their excessive self-consciousness, such as poking a bit of fun at myself after spilling some coffee. But people recoil when the object of the humor is someone else in a grave situation. A version of that can happen in therapy if the therapist makes an ill-timed or poorly constructed statement in an attempt to inject playfulness. The last thing any of us wants to do in therapy is have an empathic break, which will happen if we move humor or lightheartedness front and center when someone is telling a horrible story.

Acceptance

Therapists need to be a bit like the dogs we bring into the in-school partial hospital program where I consult. They show unconditional acceptance to the kids in the program with results sometimes nothing short of dramatic. Excessively shy children start to come out of their shell; autistic children respond to dogs' gentle nuzzling.

Unconditional acceptance involves respect for the patient, and reflects the therapist's willingness to delve into whatever topics the patient brings up.

It does not mean unconditional acceptance of behaviors, but of the person. (A patient who picks up an antique in the doctor's office and smashes it to the ground shouldn't expect that action to be met with acceptance; there are real consequences to the destruction.)

There is a song from *South Pacific* called "Carefully Taught"[6] that I've used in lectures on developmental psychology. Its basic message is that bigotry doesn't just happen; it's cultivated by carefully teaching children to sort those who are "acceptable" from those who are not. Consider the converse: Kids generally have a much greater range of what they consider acceptable than adults, who have a more developed but often more constricted sense of self-awareness, social propriety, and cultural norms.

Therapy needs to reflect some of that childlike capacity. In my visits to Saroj in prison, it seems to me to be somewhat like an elementary school, in that many of the inmates' tolerance for unusual behavior seems like that of little kids. When Saroj was first incarcerated, he was at the Otisville Correctional Camp in New York. Healing, yet still periodically experiencing dissociative episodes, Saroj would sometimes come across as quite weird. But instead of mockery and meanness, for the most part Saroj received acceptance and offers of help with the challenges of daily life in his new environment. Society has already judged the people in prison; perhaps they feel less of a need to judge each other.

Acceptance helps to allay fear. All of us experience that. Even people without mental illness can have concerns about social interaction—will they like me? Will they want to talk with me?—that ironically can result in awkward social behavior, the self-fulfilling prophesy. Lack of acceptance just perpetuates a vicious cycle.

Curiosity

Maintaining an open-minded curiosity is our best safeguard against the many pitfalls that await when we "assume" (as rather playfully admonished by some clever chap who popularized a hyphenation of the word after the first three letters), I have come to believe that curiosity bears the most emphasis of the four principles of PACE. Whether by myself, by a treatment team, by a parent or a teacher, the intentional and constant exercise of curiosity opens up a whole world of possible explanations for Billy's defiant behavior or Jenny's headaches, and the opportunity for a whole new world of truly helpful responses. I think of curiosity as the will to be empathic. So curiosity yields empathy, and empathy breeds curiosity. In short, if we empty our minds of their biases and predispositions, we can really find out what's going on in the heart and the mind of the other person.

Empathy

Empathy means the ability to take the perspectives of other people from the point of view of an open curiosity about what their world is like. This is different from what's meant by the phrase "walk a mile in their shoes." That's "what would we feel if we were them." That's not empathy. Empathy is actually tuning into the emotional signals they are giving to us and then truly understanding them, rather than understanding us being them, or a projection of us being them.

Regarding the integration of alters that characterize DID, an empathic approach would be not only to the person before us, but also to the alters. Understanding not only a life from their perspective, but also why they think the way they do, why they feel the way they do. In that we avoid drawing premature conclusions about the behavior of an alter, so should we avoid drawing premature conclusions about the behavior of anyone. Remarkably, as Saroj Parida's integration proceeded, he began to voice an empathic understanding even for the prosecution, appreciating their need to respond in some definitive way to the wrongs he committed in his dissociated states of mind.

With people who dissociate, it's so easy to draw summary and oversimplified conclusions. With some of the more high-profile cases involving criminal acts, media have used such terms as "malignant narcissism," "borderline personality," and "sociopath" to describe people who dissociate. Even if technically accurate, these characterizations don't begin to reflect an understanding of the person as a person.

It's the same with the various alters of a person with DID. For healing to take place, it's essential to take an empathic approach to the alters for these reasons:

1. Understanding the perspective of each personality better leads to appreciation of why each part of the person with DID thinks and behaves in a particular way.
2. Each alter can recognize the open-minded, empathetic, unconditionally accepting approach. This is not an unconditional acceptance of each alter's behavior, but an unconditional acceptance of each as a personality.

Putting empathy into play on a daily basis is much of what gets the spotlight in chapter 8.

· 8 ·

Coming Back Home

$\mathcal{A}$n old adage holds that "home is where the heart is." In the context of our discussion, we might modify this to say, "Home is where the heart-mind is," since the trance-prone dissociating person knows the world through her heart-mind more so than her head-mind. Going "home," therefore, means moving to a place where this struggling Dionysian feels healthy about her dissociative capacity and at peace with herself in general.

For Saroj, as we have seen, a prison sentence ironically offers continued promise of healing. Because of the confined space of prison—not in the claustrophobic sense, but in the sense of well-defined, delimited space—he has circumstances that are conducive to integration. It creates a constant opportunity for him to develop skills in his core personality for dealing with the full range of emotions. His need to dissociate because of some overwhelming state of mind is steadily diminishing. He is now using humor and other evolving interpersonal skills and talents to remain "with it," even in the most challenging situations he faces. As his fear of expressing emotion diminishes, he finds himself capable of making empathic responses that his fellow inmates find very gratifying. I sometimes smile to myself as I think of the inmates as my co-therapists with Saroj, inasmuch as they return his increasing empathic outreach to them with playful, accepting, curious, empathic responses.

ACHIEVING THE GOALS OF THERAPY

The aim of treatment of DID is not necessarily integration, although there are some who would argue to the contrary. Even without integration, it

117

might be that a better understanding of the circumstances that provoke dissociation equips the person with what she needs to feel "normal." It might be that what the individual needs is a sense of control over the alters, so they don't have the opportunity to cause impairment or any kind of life-disruptive mischief. Thus, if integration is not attainable for some reason, all is not necessarily lost.

Clinicians familiar with psychiatrist Richard Kluft's work with DID might be familiar with the term *integrationalism* as it pertains to a therapeutic goal of treating a patient with DID. Those of you who haven't read *Clinical Perspectives on Multiple Personality Disorder*, a seminal work on the subject to which he contributed as both an author and editor, may have seen the term used differently. I mention this because Kluft's use of it has nothing to do with the other definitions out there in cyberspace. I've seen it used in relation to economics, religion, sociology, and veterinary medicine, just to name a few fields of study.

The Kluft definition is as follows: "Integrationalism has two forms, both of which aim to integrate the personality in the course of the overall resolution of the patient's symptoms and difficulties in living."[1] He refers to the two forms as "strategic" and "tactical." Strategic integrationalism is the main approach I've taken with Saroj. It is a process that supports Saroj's progress toward the goal of dispensing with his need for the alters. As part of that process, the wandering mind that created the alters starts to conclude that it's way too much extra effort to sustain them; confronting and expressing emotions without the help of the alters seems not only manageable, but also desirable. As Kluft says, the DID then "collapses from within."[2] Tactical integrationalism focuses more on specific therapeutic maneuvers than its strategic cousin. The tactical approach may be seen in the more highly structured treatments such as Cognitive-Behavioral Therapy.

Another approach holds that we are all divided; it's just the human norm. In the case of someone with DID, this typical state of inner voices collaborating with each other, arguing with each other, and drawing different conclusions about the same situation just goes to extremes. The therapy associated with this stance would have the goal of lessening the extreme to the point that the alters function smoothly and harmoniously enough together.

Kluft also describes an approach to therapy called *adaptationalism*, in which the priority is helping patients manage their lives more smoothly and function more effectively. Basically, the aim is to just get rid of the impairment associated with having DID. This is probably the preferred mode of treatment in public mental health facilities, where there typically isn't the flexibility, expertise, or funding to spend time with a single patient on multiple occasions each week.

Finally, one approach that Kluft hotly criticizes sounds to me more like something an acting teacher rather than a mental health professional would do, although apparently some therapists have had great success with it. It's called *reparenting,* and involves treating each alter like an individual person, and through corrective emotional experiences, helping each achieve a healthier state. The thrust of Kluft's criticism is this: "When therapists subscribe to such beliefs, their use of themselves as the curative agent becomes central. Conventional therapeutic boundaries are often violated and the violations rationalized."[3] Indeed, my impression in interacting with fellow professionals over the years is that, the more unusual the psychotherapeutic technique, the more at risk are the therapist and patient for boundary violations of various sorts.

I should note that the whole field of treating DID is a relatively young one. It wasn't all that long ago that people who showed symptoms of DID were widely considered possessed by the devil. If we consider that "modern" treatment of DID involves only a few decades of serious and focused effort—DSM-III was the first of the DSM series to cover "multiple personality disorder" as such, and it was published in 1980—then it's easy to see how approaches to treatment might still be evolving. As a corollary, the goals of these different therapeutic approaches can be quite different, and in some cases might be achieved without the patient actually achieving mental health.

WHAT DOES HEALING FEEL LIKE?

Healing therapy brings with it a sense of self-awareness, that "mind's eye" that involves being more in touch with emotions, surroundings, one's own physical being, and as Saroj often points out, the ironies and paradoxes of life. This email from him is a good example of that developing sense of being "in touch."

> I cannot but help referring to how intimately I am connecting with Viktor Frankl's book *Man's Search for Meaning.*[4] It is really uncanny. Even though the intensity of what he and his colleagues faced far outweighs what we are facing [in prison], the emotions and the thought processes are exactly the same for both the inmates as well as the guards. As we discussed today, you may recall several issues that I had brought up prior to coming here as well as after my incarceration that appear in his book. But the weird thing is that I had not even read his book at that time. The parallels that I have drawn are too many to jot down in this email but I will just highlight a few salient ones: Using humor in darkest moments of despair; the belief that

healthy mind leads to healthy body and vice-versa and that poor mental hygiene can lead to physical catastrophe (for example, lowered body immunity); smallest of things giving the greatest of pleasures, (for example, how to get an extra piece of chicken for dinner and actually accomplishing the task would give me limitless joy).

As part of their growing self-awareness as they get better, Becky, Christa, and Saroj have noted a newfound ability to sense when they are about to dissociate, similar to the way some people can sense that a seizure or migraine headache is coming on. They can take steps to avert it. I strongly suspect this is because feelings that had formerly been shunted off into an alter have now become more tolerable as they are integrating. They can accept those feelings in their core and have a dawning awareness of circumstances that evoke them. For example, Maryann was with Christa and Zoey when Zoey needed to leave the house to do errands. Christa's fear of abandonment started to creep in, and she articulated her sense that she was about to dissociate. Becky's husband notes the same response from her on occasion when he has to go to work. She calls it a "fear of loneliness." In DID as in many other mental illnesses, the person's discovery of the emotional meaning of physical sensations greatly facilitates healing. Our awareness of this linkage is reflected in the many uses in our language of physical sensations to represent feelings: "That makes my heart sing!" (joy); "He's a pain in the neck!" (anger—of course, some substitute other anatomical regions, depending on the company kept at the time); "Thinking of that makes my guts crawl" (fear).

It's important to note that therapy has helped Becky identify the difference between the onset of a PTSD episode and the dissociation that characterizes DID. She reports that she can feel both of them coming on, but a PTSD-related flashback is associated with a "sweaty, nervous, shaky feeling" and sometimes a headache, whereas the DID is "more of a scared feeling" as in the fear of loneliness she sometimes feels when Doug has to leave the house.

Detecting oncoming dissociation happens in more ways than an internal feeling. Christa, Becky, and Saroj have an awareness of other people showing concern, or as Becky says, "I notice Doug is watching me in a particular way." The fact that they are tuned in to the empathic responses of others is just one more sign of healing, and is another example of a truism I like to emphasize especially with young psychiatry residents in training: There is a social dimension to virtually every mental illness. The mind is ultimately a social organ. Doug and Becky have also noticed that their German shepherd named Max seems to detect when Becky is about to dissociate. There is a good deal of anecdotal evidence suggesting that trained medical alert dogs can play a critical role in detecting oncoming seizures; I've also seen their remarkable sensitivity with children in the in-school partial hospital program where I consult, so Becky's experience with Max doesn't surprise me. It's an excellent example of a patient's use of existing social or environmental cues within a therapeutic approach intended to minimize the impairment caused by the DID. Through the observations of her therapist, Christa has also come to realize that she grips something like the arm of a chair or a door frame when her alter named Judge is about to emerge.

Saroj sent his reflections to Maryann on "what does healing feel like?" in December 2011, just as we were determining the flow of this chapter, and almost 18 months after Saroj had entered the prison system. His comments about internal changes and the internal and external challenges he faced are focused on the experiences of carrying a program of treatment and a healing mentality into a prison environment. For that reason, they provide unique insights about what someone with DID feels like when his mental health is improving.

It is interesting and very important to note that the realization of the benefits to my healing and everything associated with it came in a very spontaneous manner, from deep within my soul—like an "awakening." It has become abundantly clear to John and to me that my incarceration has been a true blessing in disguise that has literally saved my life so that my children would still have a father. Apparently, the alters had the foresight to see this well before I could. In fact, a lot of decisions have apparently taken place in my life, the reasoning behind which my conscious mind had not recognized at the time, but they would become rather clear later, even to me.

Here are the highlights:

1. One of the most significant experiences is that I saw my "inner family" projected onto the "outer family"—the prison environment— both singularly and plurally. What I mean by that is that I see my alters (both good and bad) being projected on to the inmates. And, by accepting them in the outer world, I am in effect embracing my inner personalities in my inner world, thereby helping in the integration process.[5]

2. Another recurring experience that has helped me tremendously in my healing is the spontaneous conversion of negatives into positives. Forcing a positive thought to justify a negative is ineffective. Spontaneous conversion always takes place. How long it takes is unpredictable, but it is definitely worth the wait. The inner satisfaction at the end of the process is unparalleled. In fact, the bigger the triggering negative [factor], the bigger the ultimate positive outcome—the reward.[6] It seems that any time I am exposed to anything negative, be it a comment or an action, somehow a positive slant comes out of

it spontaneously without me actively looking for it. I am not forcing myself into a positive outcome either as a justification or a coping mechanism. Therefore, I know from deep within me that I am not forcing it. It is happening almost as an automatic process. Therefore, paradoxically, I welcome negatives just so that I can benefit from the positives which are in fact much bigger in magnitude than the negatives that precipitated them in the first place. Isn't that interesting? Sometimes, I wonder if my belief that everything happens for a reason applies to this phenomenon also.

3. Using a physical analogy (as I did with John at a recent visit), I feel almost as though the distance separating the alters in an imaginary physical setting in my mind is narrowing almost in a palpable way. John has suggested that this is "integration," a move in the right direction.

4. I had a few symptoms when I was in Otisville Camp. I went into several trance episodes, clearly dissociated states at times, taking food stuff without my awareness and placing at places I could not recall later. In fact, Dr. M [prison psychologist] had to be called emergently on one of the episodes. The symptoms have become less frequent and less intense.

5. My appetite is legendary in prison, like folklore. I can out-eat anybody in the camp, guys much bigger than me. How can this guy do it, they wonder . . ! People even make fun of it. That is, before they realize that I am actually eating for more than one person (first person plural).[7] Even then, some cannot understand and continue to be skeptical and continue to poke fun.[8]

6. Some people make fun of my illness. It was common knowledge in Otisville, but not so in Lewisburg since the latter is a much bigger camp (one of the biggest in the country). I have learned from my mistakes in letting others know of my illness in a jail setting and also that the inmate population dynamic is very much different here. It used to bother me initially, but I accepted it and when I did, I started feeling much better about myself, all of myself. One of the standard jokes when there was a bad count [routine roll call to ensure no escapees] was: "Oh, the CO (Correction Officer) forgot to count all of Doc's personalities." Thank God, they think I have only four. So the blame is less. Imagine if they knew it was actually at least thirteen. Nevertheless, I laugh it off.

7. As I have healed, I have been able to feel the actual process of dissociation taking place, as though in slow motion and that I have some control over the process to some degree. I get very quiet and isolate myself into a remote corner (there really isn't any remote corner in jail so, the remotest possible one if there is any such thing). You may recall that I was not endowed with any tools in my social toolbox. So isolating myself is not difficult and does not draw attention.

8. A lot of my talents which I never thought I had have come out in prison and are flourishing. My thoughts have become much more free-flowing. Often I feel as though there is a volcano inside of me, full of ideas to help people, just waiting to erupt.

9. John and I have talked about the benefits of imprisonment, both mental and physical. In fact, a friend of mine met him when he visited me here and alluded to the same thing unprompted. John and I have joked about prescribing a small prison stint for everyone!

10. I am in a better shape physically than I ever was. As you know, there is mind-body connectedness: A healthy mind breeds a healthy body and vice versa.

11. I had to go cold turkey on my heavy drinking and smoking habits upon incarceration. Despite being rather uncomfortable initially—with withdrawal symptoms—it has been very good in the long run.

12. Jail life is full of improvisations and compromises, which has helped me in my healing since the alters have to cooperate with each other and work harmoniously due to the underlying "fear" factor: They have to be in synch to hide the chaos and turmoil going on inside.

13. Having a high trance capacity or dissociative capacity has been a true blessing since I am not here mentally most of the time even though I am here physically, locked up. I have traveled the universe and back many a time and revisited my favorite abodes.

14. Every time I hear negative comments from inmates about jail and everything associated with it, on top of having to hear constantly what a waste of my talent and education it is to be locked up here, serving food or scrubbing the floor, or teaching art or GED, etc., I begin to wonder if it is true. Then, immediately I realize that I am actually in the right place mentally, judged by the quality of inner peace I am experiencing. So, the physical location of where I am becomes irrelevant. I may be the only one in the prison feeling that way. Pretty crazy . . . eh!! That is my life in a nutshell.

15. I was joking with John about how upside down my life is. Even coffee makes me sleepy. My brain must be upside down.

16. I look so happy and peaceful in prison that it has prompted inmates to make comments: in Otisville, "Doc, you should ask the judge to increase your sentence," and in Lewisburg, "Doc, I thought your sentence was for two months but was surprised to learn that it was eight years."

17. I am acquiring normal human emotions more and more. I choke up sometimes during my phone conversations with my kids or John or Maryann. I even get very teary-eyed watching movies. I could not cry before. Acquisition of human emotions comes with a price: I experience more emotional pain as a result. Ongoing integration also adds to it by not allowing painful emotions to get split off into alters or not allowing spontaneous dissociation to take place.

18. The prison experience is like an elementary or middle school kid learning to live with others and experiencing normal human interactions. Personally, I consider this a wonderful human research lab that cannot be mimicked on the street, a lab where I observe all kinds of idiosyncrasies of human behavior including my own. It is a true blessing and that has also contributed to my healing in an exponential way.

FOCUS ON PURL

Friends, family, a therapist, and from Saroj's remarks, even fellow prison inmates can bring an added and critical dimension to the treatment elements of playfulness, acceptance, curiosity and empathy—love. For that reason, I'd suggest that a more complete acronym to represent the necessary treatment approach for DID would be PLACE, rather than PACE.

Actually, the idea of inserting the "L" in his PACE was my colleague Dan Hughes's idea. But at this point his impression is that the psychotherapeutic community is not ready to think about love as an active ingredient in therapy. To be sure, many excellent therapists would find it very difficult to imagine how loving their patients would take practical form without violating therapeutic boundaries or losing focus on the intent of the treatment in the first place. But I'm convinced of two things in this regard: First, it is routine for our affection for our patients to radiate through the well-kept boundaries and purposes of good therapy. Secondly, if it doesn't, the patient will sense the absence of our affection and at best will be distracted by that absence. The therapist who tries desperately to conceal his healthy affection for his patient in the name of "therapeutic neutrality" does no service for either his patient or himself.

If love is an indispensable component of good therapy, it most certainly must be present in the therapeutic interaction that family and friends have with someone under treatment for DID. For example, when Becky feels herself about to dissociate, Doug puts his arms around her and holds her tight. He assures her that she will be all right. And with that display of love, sometimes he adds a dose of playfulness: "He might change the subject and bring some humor to the moment when I feel myself drifting away," says Becky. Christa also reports that Zoey's hugs at a moment when dissociation is imminent will help her "stay together."

So as I alluded to in the previous chapter, I fully support Dr. Hughes's contention that PACE is just as helpful a guideline for family and friends as it is for clinicians—except that for family and friends I would indeed proceed straightaway to add the "L." Let me expand a bit on what it means and how it looks for us as friends and relatives of a person with DID, or with any serious mental illness for that matter, to regard them with PLACE. The following four virtues emanating from PLACE are my distillation of the wonderful reflections of the several persons with dissociative disorders whose stories have been shared in this book, and their friends and relatives.

One of the "fruits of the spirit" that PLACE requires is *patience*. Doug mentioned that he "could have called the cops" on a regular basis when he and Becky were first married, which was prior to her diagnoses of PTSD and DID. Becky's rage would flare up with a trigger like a particular noise or a smell. But he had some sense of how she had been through hell with her first husband, someone she had married at the age of fourteen. He knew a little about how she had gone from an abusive childhood to an abusive adolescence, victimized by two different violent and controlling men. And so, he decided to be patient. This was a second marriage for both, and a strong friendship had preceded their union. His patience was sustained by his curiosity to know what was causing these outbursts, since they clearly had nothing to do with their relationship. It was more difficult for Saroj's wife to exercise patience since she faced an acute situation: confiscation of assets and impending incarceration of her husband while trying to raise three young children. No one could blame her for being impatient—especially not really knowing what caused Saroj's criminal behavior—but I saw how profoundly that worked against him early in therapy. Much to her credit, she shifted gears when she realized the severity of Saroj's mental illness.

The second of these is *understanding*. Understanding is the element that allows patience to take root and both respect and loyalty to flourish. The deepest understanding comes from participation in therapy sessions, so that the clinician has an opportunity not only to educate a loved one about the disorder, but also to inform him of the rationale for the therapeutic approach. Christa and Becky are fortunate to have spouses who attend therapy sessions.

Christa also had the unique experience of a week-long series of sessions involving her spouse and parents—a unique situation since it was her parents who played a central role in the trauma she experienced as a child. After five weeks at Sierra Tucson, a psychiatric hospital in Arizona, Christa's parents and Zoey participated in family week, during which time they learned about Christa's dissociative identity disorder. "They went through a kind of intensive training to understand what people with DID are going through," says Christa.

Saroj's story in prison bears evidence to the therapeutic power of the third virtue: *respect*. H. L. Mencken defined self-respect as "the secure feeling that no one, as yet, is suspicious." To twist it a bit, we might say it's the delusion that others don't know how insecure we feel about ourselves. To me that riddle means that we are all called upon as members of the human race to tender respect to each other as fellow members, regardless of how much or how little we "esteem" the other. Saroj's integration has been greatly aided by many of his fellow inmates and several of the guards who have consistently shown him respect, whether he was teaching an art class at the time or slipping into an alter and behaving bizarrely. And I would be remiss in not adding a personal observation of respect shown Saroj by a perhaps rather unlikely source: the lead investigator for the FBI. This man was present along with me at Saroj's sentencing hearing. He not only showed warm respect directly to Saroj, but after the hearing expressed to me his positive regard for Saroj in a brief exchange on the elevator. But above all, it is the spiritually uplifting and emotionally fulfilling moments with his wife and his three young children when they visit him in prison that Saroj describes to me as being transported out of this world to a land of peace that continues to have the maximum therapeutic impact on his healing.

Finally, PLACE for the family and friends engenders *loyalty*. In a way, in persons with DID, the host's loyalty to her alters enables them to return loyalty to her, making ultimate integration more attainable and at least reducing the tension in the inner "family." So it is hardly a stretch to recognize that the loyalty the sufferer feels from loved ones will have a significant therapeutic impact. Again I think of Saroj's experience, this time of visits in prison from friends back home who would drive over three hours to see him. They remained steadily loyal to him from the moment of his arrest.

At risk of burdening you with acronym soup, it occurs to me that patience, understanding, respect and loyalty can be captured by PURL. So if you wish, you are welcome to add this PURL of wisdom to PLACE.

IS THERE ANYTHING TO FEAR?

A loved one's desire to help someone with DID can be tempered by a fear that an alter might emerge and threaten harm. I have heard many stories of (and personally experienced) alters lashing out verbally at others and, commonly, at least one alter seems rage-filled. Becky has Mean One and Inga. Christa has Judge. In Saroj's case, he had two fierce alters with the names Randy and Ravana. Randy is a homonym for "evil woman" and Ravana is a god of anger.

How likely is it that an alter would commit a physical act of violence, though? Of these three cases, there is only one instance in their collective history (that we know of, at least) in which an attack on another person occurred. One night, Becky woke up screaming, but was unaware of it until later when her husband Doug told her about it. She was also oblivious to the fact that she had scratched her husband's face. Simply to protect himself, he'd pushed her away. The bang of her head against the headboard abruptly brought her back to the moment. She looked at him in horror asking, "What happened to you?" when she saw his bleeding face. With the help of her therapist, Becky concluded that what happened was probably related to her PTSD and not, in fact, an episode of dissociation. In technical terms, DID is a post-traumatic psychopathology, and PTSD and DID sometimes coexist. A person like Becky can sometimes manifest symptoms of PTSD, therefore, without at the moment manifesting dissociative symptoms associated with DID, such as the emergence of an alter.

I believe that it would be difficult for persons with *true* DID to commit violent crimes. Developmentally speaking, it seems to me that there has to be fundamental personality integration before the personality can disintegrate into alters. In other words, somewhat paradoxically, research suggests that dissociative potential comes out of a state of integration.[9] One core feature of an integrated personality is a healthy conscience. Development of conscience goes hand in hand with the initial achievement of an integrated personality in early childhood. To balance this assertion with hypothesis from others,[10] I should note that some studies have linked pathological dissociation with violent behavior by looking at prison inmates who suffered from dissociative disorders, including diagnosed cases of DID. It's extremely important to note, however, that they cited factors such as "significant emotional arousal and alcohol use"[11] as playing a role when the crimes were committed.

People who are more violence-prone in the absence of states of intoxication or brain damage tend to have personalities that never achieved that initial integration. Of the three basic types of unintegrated personalities, the most likely to engage in gratuitous violence is referred to as the *antisocial personality*. A lay synonym is simply "sociopath." While those suffering from the other two types, the narcissistic personality and the borderline personality, can at least at times see some good in the world or in themselves, the person with antisocial personality cannot. These are the persons for whom life is miserable and meaningless, and so, "While I'm alive I'll just eat my lunch and everyone else's I can get my hands on." And their credo sadly adorns their bumper: "Life sucks, and then you die."

Persons with borderline personality disorder vacillate between states of mind wherein they feel radically good or radically bad, and wherein they see the world similarly. They are also prone to episodes of destructive behavior, although usually not with the frequency or intensity of the antisocial person.

Nevertheless, because of the relative prevalence of persons with borderline personality, it is not surprising that a study by the University of Iowa's Department of Psychiatry concluded, "Borderline personality disorder is relatively common among both male and female offenders in prison."[12]

SOCIETY'S CHILDREN

Bring up the subject of multiple personalities in a social setting and you are likely to have at least one person in the room assert strongly, "That's ridiculous!" Many people don't believe someone can be driving a car on a road they have traveled for years and suddenly not remember where they are. They don't believe someone can commit insurance fraud and have no idea what he did or where the money was deposited. They don't believe an intelligent woman can have personalities that convince everyone around her she is mentally retarded.[13]

Tell the same group of people about experiences of a PTSD sufferer returning from a war with flashbacks, depression, or alcoholism, and they will be appropriately sympathetic. It's so much easier to appreciate the mind-bending effects of exploding roadside bombs and the severed limbs of comrades. Unfortunately, we in the community of mental health professionals haven't done a good enough job of making it clear that PTSD isn't just a war-related pathology. It can result from severe trauma in childhood, and those sufferers can also have flashbacks, depression, and/or self-medicate with alcohol and drugs. Inflict that trauma on a child who is highly trance-prone and the result is Christa, Becky, and Saroj—people who sometimes don't remember both ordinary and significant things, and who might behave as though "they just aren't themselves." On top of that, they might also self-medicate, have flashbacks, and feel depressed.

Christa, Becky, and Saroj are healing because they are very, very fortunate. Each one has the benefit of therapy a couple of times a week (Saroj and I now continue to connect via both phone and visits while he is in prison) and they all have loved ones who consistently exhibit patience, understanding, respect, and loyalty. But what about others, forced by economic constraints to rely on public services?

Persons with PTSD and dissociative disorders in our current society are at double jeopardy for inadequate treatment: the dilemma of our pervasive lack of adequate understanding of the nature and prevalence of the disorders is compounded by severely limited funding for mental health services for those without good health insurance plans or dependent on a meagerly funded public mental health system. We just can't expect to "bring people home" who suffer from one or both of them by limiting necessary access to well-trained clinicians or by substituting medication for it.

And we can't bring them home by failing to redouble our nascent efforts to bring good mental health care into our prisons. I believe that the very name "Department of Corrections" embodies that spirit. I am seeing firsthand in Saroj's prison experience the same reality that I experienced as a former Marine officer, as a physician in training, and as a psychiatrist dealing at times with hostile aggressive children and adults: a tough-minded expectation for responsible accountability for misbehavior is most successfully administered in the spirit of P(L)ACE. I am more convinced than ever that appropriate legal constraints on the freedom of offenders, when combined creatively with sound mental health principles and practices, will ultimately yield immeasurable savings in societal distress and in dollars and cents. To this end, the mental health community needs to give up the plea of "not guilty by reason of insanity." And the corrections system needs to give up the bias toward punishment over correction, especially when it comes to criminals who are mentally ill. It doesn't mean letting them off the hook: The best way to perpetuate a person's inappropriate behavior is to relieve him of responsibility for it. It means responding with intelligence and empathy to the reality that a disproportionately high percentage of people in prison suffer from some kind of mental illness.

FINDING SANITY

Comrades in prison comment to Saroj how congenial he is to everyone; how he has returned rude behavior with kindness, empathy, and compassion. That has impressed other inmates; they openly ask about this capacity, particularly knowing that he had been diagnosed with a serious mental illness.

In recognizing in others the negative emotions he has had to learn to tolerate in his alters, Saroj has grown into this ability to respond patiently and respectfully to them when those negative emotions are directed his way. And he finds that they then tend to reciprocate.

Let me end with this observation. Before his arrest, intensive treatment, and imprisonment, Saroj was considered an oddball by people who interacted with him professionally and personally—a brilliant physician oddball. He has become a warm, sensitive, gracious person in the course of his ongoing integration in prison. But he may well emerge at the end of his sentence as a warm, sensitive, gracious oddball. My point is this: There are seven billion or so different personalities in this world. Among them are several billion won-derful people who are somewhat odd. Some of them are cloyingly theatrical. Some of them are dour. Some of them are too verbose, and some of them too quiet. But they are wonderful nevertheless. The more we tolerate the idiosyncrasy in our fellow man, the less we mistake it as mental illness—and the less mental illness there will be.

Look for the sanity of the people in your life, and you will find it.

Epilogue

$\mathcal{A}$t around the time I completed the writing of this book, I met with a patient—an engaging and articulate young man—who I've been treating for some time for bouts of anxiety and depression. As usual, medication has been helpful but insufficient to yield more enduring relief. My ultimate aim in psychotherapy with my patients is to enable them to develop an ongoing, reliable ability for self-reflection: that is, the ability to be once removed "in real time" from one's thoughts, emotions, memories, and interactions with others, as though he were just outside his conscious life and looking in. To my delight, the young man described a recent, sudden, and significant plummet in his mood as follows: "It came on quite suddenly, after the semester ended and before Christmas. I couldn't identify any cause. But I said to myself, 'Here goes the brain chemistry again! I know I can ride this one out like the others.' I let my fiancée know what was happening, so she wouldn't take my irritability personally. It only lasted a couple of days!"

He went on to reflect how in his adolescence, when his bouts of depression began, he would be oblivious to what was happening to him and become anxious and socially uncommunicative, thereby deepening the depression. And as we reflected together on this most recent "depression," we agreed that indeed there probably *was* a plausible explanation for it: an exhaustion of those brain chemicals necessary for mood maintenance secondary to an inordinately great academic load in the just-completed semester of graduate school. Thus, my patient's ability to stand a bit outside himself enabled him to "observe" rather than "be" his depression, and thereby to contain it and prevent it from becoming complicated by anxiety. And *believe it or not*, at the very time I was writing this little vignette, my daughter called me and, not knowing what I was writing at the moment, told me that she recently underwent a sudden and surprising dip in mood. As one practicing mindfulness in the Zen tradition, she "observed" her depressed mood and called a trusted friend in order to reflect on it.

These two stories inspired me to leave the readers with some questions to ponder. Maybe some of you will find your personal mental life enriched as you do so. Maybe some of you are mental health professionals and will find your practices enriched as you seek answers. And maybe some of you are researchers who may be stimulated by the questions to pursue the answers through neuro-scientific research.

What is the relationship between self-reflection and dissociation? Are they one and the same? When we speak of the "mind's eye," are we talking about a very beneficial dissociated state of mind?

Related to these questions is one about the very common diagnosis of attention deficit hyperactivity disorder. In my years of experience with folks with this disorder I have gained the impression that they range in dissociative potential all the way from Apollonian to Dionysian, the former tending to be externally distractible and the latter internally distractible. When medication works, it seems to yield a greater capacity for reflective states of mind and therefore a greater capacity for sustained attentiveness and impulse control. However, this beneficial effect seems to be more evident in the Odysseans and Dionysians with the disorder than in the Apollonians. So, in adequately treating persons with attention deficit hyperactivity disorder, are we enhancing their potential to use their dissociative capacity? Can this be demonstrated via brain imaging studies? If self-reflection and self-monitoring are related to dissociative capacity, how can we best help people with low dissociative capacity to become more self-reflective? As patients gain greater ability to maintain an ongoing state of partially dissociated self-reflection, are they then able to decrease or discontinue their need for medication?

Finally, allow me to remind you of my introductory hope that you'd find a story in this book, one that may "stick" with you. As for me, the moral of the Saroj Parida story is that our legal and criminal justice systems and our mental health systems need to join forces ever more intentionally and enthusiastically as we evolve as a culture. And I believe that this will be one salient hallmark of our progress. Truly, Saroj has benefited substantially from several features of his life in prison. While there is plenty to be improved upon in our criminal justice system, there is also a lot that's *right* about it, with some very good people and some very helpful practices. I am convinced that we can distill the "active ingredients" of the prison experience that have been so helpful for Saroj, and creatively develop ways to provide them for other persons with (or without) mental illness who are sentenced to prison. The humanitarian benefits of this effort alone would make the effort worthwhile. But I believe that in the final analysis what's humanitarian is also what's economically sound.

I hope you are persuaded by Saroj's story that responsibility for one's actions must never be forfeited on the basis of one's mental illness. But what follows then is that our criminal justice efforts via departments of corrections must then continue to aim to create prison environments richly informed by state-of-the-art understandings of mental illness and its various disorders, including dissociative disorders, so that for the sake of all of us, their inhabitants have the maximum chance to emerge prepared for socially as well as mentally healthy lives.

Perhaps my greatest hope in closing is that you have been inspired toward a greater fascination with this most amazing of human organs—the *mind*. For our human minds navigate in an awesome ongoing journey throughout this boundless universe of body, spirit, and relationship that we call life. Inasmuch as I began with the matter of *belief* and *doubt*, I hope that your navigation system may contain just enough doubt that you don't trust your belief too much, and with just enough belief to enable you to keep going. Above all, enjoy the journey!

Appendix

$\mathcal{H}$ere is a summary of the stories of the three dissociative identity disorder patients mentioned in several chapters. All of them contributed a great deal to the discussion of dissociation through their candor and ability to reflect on their experiences with mind and heart fully engaged. I am pleased to note that all of them are now flourishing.

CHRISTA'S STORY

Born on Christmas Day, Christa nearly died the same day. Her parents belonged to a religious group that believed a child born on Christmas was cursed and should immediately be killed. Throughout her childhood, she not only heard that she "should have died," but also had to endure excessively stern punishment from her father, who had episodes of rage. A high school classmate raped, tortured, and mutilated her when she came to his house to tutor him in math. This vicious attack only came to light when her physician found significant internal damage on examination. Another rape—this one publicized because it was a rare event on a quiet college campus—caused her father to push her toward marriage with her high school boyfriend since she was "damaged goods." The high school boyfriend turned out to have serious antisocial behavior.

In reflecting on why she tolerated marriage for a few years to this emotionally and physically abusive man, Christa offers this:

> I didn't necessarily remember how the incidents played out, but I remembered what he tried to do. He would suffocate me until I passed out. He

135

would strangle me. He beat me, starved me, and raped me. He was playing God with my life, and eventually, he thought he was God and told me so.

Christa escaped from the marriage and found substantial success in business. Colleagues may have noticed she had unusual memory lapses and perhaps oddly quiet or oddly angry behavior at times, but they likely dismissed it. No doubt, they concluded that she was so smart and productive, there couldn't be anything seriously wrong with her.

Eventually, Christa found Zoey, and they legally sealed their marriage vows when same-sex couples were first able to do so. During the course of their relationship, Zoey would sometimes wonder about the memory lapses, but both of them attributed the amnesia to a scuba diving accident during which Christa had gotten Type 2 decompression sickness ("the bends"), which affects the brain. It was another aspect of Christa's behavior that aroused tremendous concern in Zoey, though, because it involved spontaneous outbursts.

> All of a sudden, a conversation would take a turn that didn't make any sense to me. I would stop and say to Christa, "What is this? Is this really about me? This isn't making sense to me." It wasn't nonsense, but simply tangential to what we'd been talking about. The tangent would always be accusatory or confrontational, so it wasn't just a matter of changing the subject.

Christa entered the Sierra Tucson psychiatric facility in Arizona for an intense, eight-week treatment involving their specialists in post-traumatic pathology. The daily sessions and evaluations led to the diagnosis of both PTSD and DID. The alters they identified are known simply as Silent One and Judge. It was likely Silent One who took over when Christa's husband abused her, and Judge who came to the fore with spontaneous rage.

While at Sierra Tucson, Christa—a gifted artist—painted a portrait of Judge. It appears to be the profile of the front half of a gray wolf. A fierce stare, combined with long fangs and teeth interlocked and bared in a growl, suggest the intent to kill. The wolf's thick, sharp claws are red, as though covered with blood. Four parallel slits of roughly equal size on the shoulder suggest that something recently attacked it and drew blood. When Christa completed the painting and held it up, the people she showed it to remarked that it looks as though Judge is coming out of her abdomen or out of the side of her. Christa says, "Silent One doesn't have any pictures. It's more like nothingness than an entity."

Christa has been going to therapy twice weekly since that diagnosis, and she and Zoey have a joint therapy session each week as well. Christa still dissociates, but not as much, and she and Zoey have found ways to prevent episodes, primarily by consistently showing trusting, caring behavior.

BECKY'S STORY

Becky's first round of abuse began when she was in kindergarten and continued until she was eight years old. So typical for children at that age, she concluded that she somehow deserved the beatings and sexual assault; she assumed it was because God considered her a bad girl. Her only friend as a child was an imaginary girl named Berberlishes, who had blue eyes and long brown hair and always wore dresses.

Becky's mother finally stopped the abuse by divorcing Becky's father. But it took a lot to bring her to that point: One night, armed with a rifle, he threatened to shoot everyone in the family. The only thing that stopped him was that Becky's older brother had the strength to knock him down.

At the age of fourteen, Becky married a local eighteen-year-old boy with her mother's blessing. For a brief period after the wedding Becky's husband seemed normal. She soon became pregnant, and he began to emotionally abuse her during the pregnancy. She remembers having thought, "This is my life." After the birth of the child, her husband began to physically abuse her also.

After one incident in which he knocked her down a flight of stairs, she heard the voices—several of them—tell her to get help. She went to one session with a therapist, but didn't go back because of the severe beating she received as punishment when she returned home.

Strange things started to happen. She once woke up with bruises on her face and thought, once again, she'd been victimized by her spouse. For a change, he hadn't been the abuser; she'd done it to herself. Becky also recalls instances eerily similar to those self-mutilation experiences described by Cameron West in his book *First Person Plural*. She had the sense of looking down on herself from the ceiling while she beat and stabbed herself. In her case, the alter crying out for help was a middle-aged woman she soon knew only as The Mother. She has long red hair.

Finally extricating herself from the abusive relationship, she found Doug, a wonderful man who'd been a friend to her in the darkest times and to whom she is currently married. But the odd behavior continued. One night she woke up screaming, but was unaware of it: "I was unconscious of the fact that I was screaming." She was also oblivious to the fact that she had scratched her husband's face, causing him to bleed profusely. Simply to protect himself, he'd pushed her away. The bang of her head against the headboard abruptly stopped the dissociation. She looked at his bloody face in horror asking, "What happened to you?"

Doug and Becky sought help. When Becky finally entered therapy, her therapist ordered the usual diagnostic tests to determine if there were organic issues. What they found shocked Becky, but would not surprise those aware of the chronic brain changes that can occur as a result of childhood trauma. Scans indicated irregularities in certain regions of her brain—recall the changes referenced above that can be triggered by the excessive release of stress hormones during trauma. Further, IQ tests showed her to be in the genius category.

But what had been Becky's favorite job? She had excelled at her hands-on job in a plastics factory. It was physically demanding and repetitive work; it required relatively little thinking. This was the job she held while in the abusive relationship and she loved it. Her work environment involved supportive, caring people; she had a secure, happy place to which to retreat five days a week for respite from the abuse.

Becky plunged into depression when the onset of rheumatoid arthritis made it impossible for her to continue in that job. In discussing the loss later with her therapist, she wondered how she could have enjoyed that job so much when she supposedly had such a brilliant intellect. "It was your coping strategy," said the therapist. To me, this is just one more instance of how miraculously the mind can pull us through trauma and offer us hope and protection during the darkest times. (Similarly, we can look at Saroj's period of incarceration as a coping strategy devised by an alter that recognized the need for a stable, predicable environment.)

Becky now knows that she and Doug had to share their home with Berberlishes; Mean One; The Mother; a man who speaks only French; Inga, the one who is "always pissed off"; and a middle-aged woman who is like Becky, but far more sexually daring. Sometimes, they have conversations among themselves that she can hear, although she admits that she really doesn't understand the guy who speaks French, even though she studied it in high school.

As a way to reach out to others with PTSD and DID, Becky wrote and self-published a fictionalized account of her life called *My Broken Wings*. Her two aims: first, to tell people help is not only available, but it is also "all over the place"; and second, to make it clear that you can't heal by yourself. She's right, of course. Reading books about these disorders, talking to supportive friends and relatives, and spiritual pursuits can be very helpful. But the mental aspect of PTSD and DID is so complex that a specialized psychotherapeutic approach invariably is necessary and constitutes the core of the healing effort.

SAROJ'S STORY

When Saroj Parida was four years old, his parents brought a twelve-year-old boy to live with them as a household servant. It was common practice in India, even among families without much means. Saroj's parents were young and wanted to get out and enjoy themselves. They had already sent their firstborn to live with his maternal grandmother and, with the house-boy under their roof, they now had someone to care for Saroj as well. Worried that his parents might go away for a long time like his older brother—or maybe not come back at all—he would become very anxious when his parents would leave. The houseboy would soothe him by stroking his legs. For the next few years, the fondling progressed from playful touching to rape—and the threats progressed from "this is our secret" to "you tell and it will be the last thing you do."

Saroj's academic accomplishments separated him from fellow students and, at an early age, put him in the company of high-powered people in academic circles. For example, when he was twelve, he was awarded the National Science Talent Scholarship and ranked ninth in the entire country of India. That year, he was also picked as the youngest school student to represent his state at a national science convention held in New Delhi. Only two students were picked from each state to assemble in the capital and meet the then-prime minister Indira Gandhi. And at the age of fifteen, he was awarded acceptance into one of the top medical schools in India. Throughout his childhood his father meted harsh, physical punishments for failures on any level while publicly demonstrating great pride in his genius son.

Saroj graduated medical school at age twenty-one and entered a pediatric residency, which led immediately to a research position in England followed by a fellowship position at the University of Kentucky. He then went to the University of Pittsburgh and worked in a neonatal intensive care unit. A string of professional successes followed, as did a marriage to a beautiful Indian American woman named Anju. They had three children while he continued to publish prolifically and do research. Desiring to spend more time with his family, he moved to an environment where he could minimize research duties, and instead, focus on patient care. It was during this time that he earned a reputation as "the infant whisperer" because of the uncanny way he seemed to connect with babies and bring them back to life and health. Concurrently, in an effort to spend more time with his own children, he began an in-home consulting practice.

Saroj had long been plagued by inept social behaviors, but they started to worsen, and included routine failure at simple tasks like parking his car in the correct spot in the hospital staff lot and remembering the names of persons with whom he had played golf several times. He had thoughts of suicide to the point of once borrowing a gun, and frequently parking his car at the edge of a quarry.

And then on February 26, 2009, the authorities paid a visit. A car pulled into the Parida driveway on a street lined with stone mini-mansions. Two gentlemen in long black overcoats rushed from the car to the Parida's front door. Saroj was sitting in his study, his back to a photo of Tiger Woods on the green. They rang the bell; he opened the door as Anju walked into the room. The men identified themselves as agents and asked Saroj and Anju if there was anybody else in the house and whether they had any weapons. The men announced they had come from the Attorney General's office and represented the federal government. In a fog, Saroj asked innocently, "Why are you here?" He had no idea he had filed more than $7 million in fraudulent insurance claims.

A little more than a week later, Saroj was referred to me for evaluation by a psychiatrist friend of his attorney. His chief complaint: "I'm so confused about what I've been doing these past two years. I must have lost my mind." How could Saroj not have suspected that he needed help?

It really had to take a calamity for Saroj to get into treatment because, paradoxically, it was his mental illness that enabled him to function relatively normally all those years. Saroj was like anyone else: Once human beings learn to adapt to compensate for or cope with a situation, we don't want to *un*-adapt. Saroj was holding on to what worked so he had no reason to say, "I think I'll go into therapy and see if there's anything wrong with me."

Within a few months, I became familiar with most of the rest of Saroj's "family":

- **Infant** and/or **Baby,** who would sometimes surface when there was the need to express an emotion like "even if you're displeased with me, you won't hurt someone so small and helpless"
- **Sissy,** who is about five or six years old; Sissy was the only one who would contact my coauthor, Maryann
- **Teenager,** who has an odd and impressive appetite; even in prison, Saroj has a reputation for eating far beyond what seems reasonable and not gaining weight
- **Randy Gonzalez,** one of his "assistants" who committed the insurance fraud and affixed his signature to many of the claims; the name Randy is a homonym for the Hindi word meaning "evil woman"
- **Ravi,** another assistant in the scheme; the name that means "sun"
- **Kumar,** the third "assistant," but he was fired by the other two when he apparently opposed chaotic billing practices

- **Ravana**, the angry personality
- **Giver** and/or **Diya Babu**, the latter being the Hindi phrase referring to "the giver"; ultimately this pregenital identity became fused with a desire to give women sexual pleasure
- **Inventor**, a late-emerging alter who encouraged him tell his story to the world
- **Protector**, an alter who angrily repudiated him for not defending his "internal family" from challenges
- **Destroyer**, an alter with a presence since childhood

Saroj jokes that he's never really been home alone: He always has his "family" inside his head.

On July 19, 2010, Saroj walked into a federal prison camp, a correctional facility primarily for nonviolent offenders, and the guarded doors closed behind him. Since then, he has flourished. We continue to have brief weekly sessions on the phone and visits whenever possible. But the real healing on a day-to-day basis comes from his interaction with the other inmates. They accept him, they appreciate his talents, and they show real caring for him. The prison system itself provides a structure and predictability that benefits him at this stage of his healing. In that his imprisonment literally appears as an inevitable outcome of his illness and provides necessary facets of his treatment, Saroj and I have speculated that his alters may have engineered his incarceration—in essence an ironic case of unconscionable acts as acts of conscience. Taking a bird's eye view of his life story, I can allow for this possibility. The cost of his crimes to himself, his family, and society has been substantial. But the cost of his having proceeded further unchecked with his deteriorating professional and personal life would have been even more substantial. And the potential benefits of his sharing his story with fellow sufferers, mental health professionals, policy makers in the legal and criminal justice fields, and the citizenry at large are inestimable.

Saroj has already used his newfound sense of healing and integration to communicate with people about disorders involving trauma and dissociation, including other DID patients like Becky, whose story is also included here. As a doctor and as a patient, he reaches out with empathy.

Notes

FOREWORD

1. Debbie Nathan, *Sybil Exposed* (New York: Free Press, 2011).

CHAPTER 1

1. Charles Dodson, a.k.a. Lewis Carroll, *Through the Looking Glass* (ebook), Project Gutenberg, www.gutenberg.org/.

2. Kalina Christoff, Alan M. Gordon, Jonathan Smallwood, Rachelle Smith, and Jonathan W. Schooler, "Experience Sampling during fMRI Reveals Default Network and Executive System Contributions to Mind Wandering," *Proceedings of the National Academy of Sciences of the United States* 106, no. 21(May 2009), 8719, doi:10.1073/pnas.0900234106.

3. Herbert Spiegel and David Spiegel, *Trance and Treatment: Clinical Uses of Hypnosis*, 2nd edition (Washington, DC: American Psychiatric Publishing, 2004).

4. Anthony Robbins website, http://www.tonyrobbins.com/.

5. Jim McCormick website, http://www.takerisks.com/.

6. Jim Lagopoulos, Jian Xu, Inge Rasmussen, Alexandra Vik, Gin S. Malhi, Carl F. Eliassen, Ingrid E. Arntsen, Jardar G. Sæther, Stig Hollup, Are Holen, Svend Davanger, and Øyvind Ellingsen, "Increased Theta and Alpha EEG Activity during Nondirective Meditation," *The Journal of Alternative and Complementary Medicine* 15, no. 11 (November 2009), 1187–92, doi:10.1089/acm.2009.0113.

7. Robert B. Oxnam, *A Fractured Mind: My Life with Multiple Personality Disorder* (New York: Hyperion, 2005).

8. James Eric Eich, "The Cue-dependent Nature of State-dependent Retrieval," *Memory and Cognition* 8, no. 2 (1980), 157–73.

9. Gitta Sereny, *Cries Unheard: Why Children Kill: The Story of Mary Bell* (New York: Metropolitan Books, 1999).

10. Abbreviation for *Schutzstaffel*, translated "protection squadron."

11. Post Traumatic Stress Disorder Fact Sheet, The Sidran Institute, http://www.sidran.org/sub.cfm?contentID=66&sectionid=4.

12. A. B. Newberg and E. G. d'Aquili, "The Neuropsychology of Religious and Spiritual Experience," *Journal of Consciousness Studies* 7, nos. 11–12 (November–December 2000), 251–66.

CHAPTER 2

1. Chris Costner Sizemore and Elen Sain Pittillo, *I'm Eve* (New York: Doubleday & Co., 1977).

2. American Psychiatric Association, *Diagnostic and Statistical Manual of Mental Disorders, Fourth Edition (Text Revision)* (DSM-IV-TR; Washington, DC: American Psychiatric Publishing, July 2000).

3. Alliance of Psychodynamic Organizations, *Psychodynamic Diagnostic Manual (PDM)* (Bethesda, MD: Alliance of Psychoanalytic Organizations, 2006). The Alliance of Psychodynamic Organizations is a collaboration of the major psychoanalytic organizations including the American Psychoanalytic Association, International Psychoanalytical Association, the Division of Psychoanalysis of the American Psychological Association, American Academy of Psychoanalysis, and National Membership Committee on Psychoanalysis in Clinical Social Work.

4. Stella Chess and Alexander Thomas, *Temperament: Theory and Practice* (New York: Routledge, 1996).

5. Ward Yont, *A Funny Thing Happened on the Way to a Life Sentence* (unpublished manuscript), chapter 1.

6. Martha Stout, *The Myth of Sanity* (New York: Viking Penguin, 2001), 209–10.

7. Cecil Adams, "Why Did Mystery Writer Agatha Christie Mysteriously Disappear?" *The Straight Dope Classics*, April 2, 1982, http://www.straightdope.com/columns/read/361/why-did-mystery-writer-agatha-christie-mysteriously-disappear.

8. Otto Isakower, "A Contribution to the Psychopathology of Phenomena Associated with Falling Asleep," *International Journal of Psycho-Analysis* 19 (1938), 331–45 (original work published 1936).

9. Steve Martin, *Born Standing Up: A Comic's Life* (New York: Scribner, 2008).

10. Mary Beth Schweigert, "The Infant Whisperer," *Lancaster New Era*, February 21, 2003, D1.

CHAPTER 3

1. In contrast, thalamic pain originates in the thalamus and generates a cortical sense of pain. Usually, some kind of neurologic disorder is at the root of it.

2. A. R. Damásio, B. J. Everitt, and D. Bishop, "The Somatic Marker Hypothesis and the Possible Functions of the Prefrontal Cortex," *Philosophical Transactions of the Royal Society of London, Series B: Biological Sciences* 351, no. 1346 (October 1996), 1413–20, doi:10.1098/rstb.1996.0125.

3. Abraham Maslow, *Motivation and Personality* (New York: Harper and Row, 1954).

CHAPTER 4

1. Bessel A. van der Kolk, Alexander C. McFarlane, and Lars Weisaeth (eds.), *Traumatic Stress: The Effects of Overwhelming Experience on Mind, Body, and Society* (New York: Guilford Press, 1996), 307.

2. Paul A. Frewen and Ruth A. Lanius, "Neurobiology of Dissociation: Unity and Disunity in Mind-Body-Brain," *Psychiatric Clinics of North America* 29 (2006), 113–28.

3. Ibid., 116–117.

4. A journal article describing the scale and its value is James D. A. Parker, Graeme J. Taylor, and R. Michael Bagby, "The 20-Item Toronto Alexithymia Scale III: Reliability and Factorial Validity in a Community Population," *Journal of Psychosomatic Research* 55 (2003), 269–75, http://www.uned.es/psico-doctorado-envejecimiento/articulos/Ellgring/ParkerTAS03.pdf; versions of the self-report measure can be found at multiple sites by entering the search phrase "online alexithymia questionnaire."

5. Cameron West, *First Person Plural* (New York: Hyperion, 1999), 1–2.

6. Ibid., 241.

7. From an interview with Rebecca Young-Losee on December 11, 2011.

8. Eric Hoffer, *The True Believer: Thoughts on the Nature of Mass Movements* (New York: Harper, 2002 [first published 1951]).

9. Gregory Hartley and Maryann Karinch, *Get People to Do What You Want* (Franklin Lakes, NJ: Career Press, 2008), 69–70.

10. "Charisma," http://en.wikipedia.org/wiki/Charisma.

11. Kreskin used the term as part of his description of a board game called Kreskin's ESP, which he developed for Milton Bradley in 1966.

12. Hartley and Karinch, 72.

13. Ibid., 90.

CHAPTER 5

1. Rick Nauert, "Brain Imaging May Improve Autism Diagnosis," PsychCentral.com, June 1, 2011 (reviewed by John M. Grohol), http://psychcentral.com/news/2011/06/01/brain-imaging-may-improve-autism-diagnosis/26599.html.

2. Ellert Nijenhuis, Onno van der Hart, and Kathy Steele, "Trauma-Related Structural Dissociation of the Personality,"*Activitas Nervosa Superior* 52, no. 1 (2010), 3.

3. Eric Vermetten, Meena Vythilingam, Steven M. Southwick, Dennis S. Charney, and J. Douglas Bremner, "Long-Term Treatment with Paroxetine Increases Verbal Declarative Memory and Hippocampal Volume in Posttraumatic Stress Disorder," *Society of Biological Psychiatry* 54 (2003), 693–702.

4. Eric Vermetten, Christian Schmahl, Sanneke Lindner, Richard J. Loewenstein, and J. Douglas Bremner, "Hippocampal and Amygdalar Volumes in Dissociative Identity Disorder," *The American Journal of Psychiatry* 163, no. 4 (April 2006), 630–36.

5. John J. B. Allen and Hallam L. Movius, II, "The Objective Assessment of Amnesia in Dissociative Identity Disorder Using Event-related Potentials," *International Journal of Psychophysiology* 38 no. 1 (2000), 21–41, http://dx.doi.org/10.1016/S0167-8760(00)00128-8.

6. Stephanie Leong, Wendi Waits, and Carroll Diebold, "Dissociative Amnesia and DSM-IV-TR Cluster C Personality Traits," *Psychiatry* 3, no. 1 (January 2006), 51–55.

7. Ronald L. Kotler and Maryann Karinch, *365 Ways to Get a Good Night's Sleep* (Cincinnati: Adams Media, 2009), 62–65.

8. Content provided by Michael S. Greevy, PhD, Commonwealth Affiliates, P.C., Harrisburg, Pennsylvania, following tests conducted April 16, 2009.

9. Through Maryann's extensive work with extreme athletes, she has found that many people who could probably be classed as having hyperthymic temperaments due to their love of attention, tendency to take risks, and so on seem to go out of their way to find the most dangerous way to do something. In an overt way, they do invite trauma.

CHAPTER 6

1. Charles S. Myers, *Shell Shock in France, 1914–1918: Based on a War Diary* (reprint of the 1940 edition in paperback, Cambridge: Cambridge University Press, 2012), 66–67.

2. Ellert Nijenhuis, Onno van der Hart, and Kathy Steele, "Trauma-Related Structural Dissociation of the Personality,"*Activitas Nervosa Superior* 52, no. 1 (2010), 2, http://www.activitas.org/index.php/nervosa/article/view/81/125.

3. Ibid.

4. Mary Beth Schweigert, "The Infant Whisperer," *Lancaster New Era*, February 21, 2003, D1.

5. From an interview with Kenneth Seeley on September 24, 2011; Seeley is a Board Registered Interventionist, Level II.

6. Saroj himself made it clear to me that he does not blame the insurance companies in any way, and therefore he takes exception to our assertion here.

7. National Association of Cognitive-Behavioral Therapists, "What is Cognitive-Behavioral Therapy," n.d., NACBT Online Headquarters, http://www.nacbt.org/whatiscbt.htm.

8. Antonio Damásio: *Descartes' Error: Emotion, Reason, and the Human Brain* (New York: Penguin, 2005).

9. Leo Madow, *Love: How to Understand and Enjoy It* (New York: Macmillan, 1983), 9.

10. Daniel A. Hughes, *Attachment-Focused Family Therapy Workbook* (New York: W.W. Norton, 2011).

CHAPTER 7

1. Martha Stark, *Modes of Therapeutic Action* (Northvale, NJ: Jason Aronson), 1999.

2. Richard P. Kluft, "Basic Principles in Conducting the Psychotherapy of Multiple Personality Disorder," chapter 3 in Richard P. Kluft and Catherine G. Fine (eds.), *Clinical Perspectives on Multiple Personality Disorder* (Washington, DC: American Psychiatric Publishing, 1993), 21.

3. Ibid., 26–47.

4. Expressed by Richard Kluft as a member of the audience at The Margaret S. Mahler Psychiatric Research Foundation Symposium (Philadelphia, 2009) when asked by a member of a panel about the resolution of DID.

5. Herbert Spiegel and David Spiegel, *Trance and Treatment: Clinical Uses of Hypnosis*, second ed. (Washington, DC: American Psychiatric Publishing, 2004), 116.

6. "Carefully Taught," from *South Pacific*, sung by Mandy Patinkin. Undated YouTube video uploaded by respectanimals on January 22, 2008, http://www.youtube.com/watch?v=nHKzn8aHyXg.

CHAPTER 8

1. Richard P. Kluft, "Basic Principles in Conducting the Psychotherapy of Multiple Personality Disorder," chapter 3 in Richard P. Kluft and Catherine G. Fine (eds.), *Clinical Perspectives on Multiple Personality Disorder* (Washington, DC: American Psychiatric Publishing, 1993), 22.

2. Ibid.

3. Ibid.

4. Psychiatrist Viktor Frankl was held in four different Nazi death camps during World War II. His memoir, *Man's Search for Meaning*, which Beacon Press first published in 1959, presents intensely thought-provoking stories and insights about why some people survived—and even grew psychologically and spiritually—during their time in the concentration camps while others essentially "lost their lives" whether or not they physically died.

5. My colleagues familiar with psychoanalytic theory will be thinking here of a sort of projection-introjection cycle.

6. In his correspondence and conversations, Saroj started to have a recurring theme of "spontaneous conversion of negatives to positives." This often meant that

an incident involving a strong emotion that might have previously triggered dissociation became something he could cope with because of a newfound belief that "things would work out." One example was an incident at Otisville in which he lost a seat at the cafeteria table, but felt he "won in the long run" by gaining the support of key inmates who stood by him.

7. Saroj's reference unintentionally captured the same phrasing as the title of Dr. Cameron West's book about his own DID, *First Person Plural*, referenced earlier.

8. As a physician I frankly struggle to understand how this is physiologically possible. But amazingly, Saroj is an extremely fit, slender man of average height, with very little body fat. So if I am to practice what I preached in the introduction, I must not resolve my doubt by clinging to comfortable, conventional medical disbelief.

9. Stephanie Leong, Wendi Waits, and Carroll Diebold, "Dissociative Amnesia and DSM-IV-TR Cluster C Personality Traits," *Psychiatry* 3, no. 1 (January 2006), 51–55, http://www.ncbi.nlm.nih.gov/pmc/articles/PMC2990548/.

10. Andrew Moskowitz, "Dissociation and Violence: A Review of the Literature," *Trauma, Violence, and Abuse* 5, no. 1 (January 2004), 21–46.

11. Ibid.

12. D. W. Black, T. Gunter, J. Allen, N. Blum, S. Arndt, G. Wenman, and B. Sieleni, "Borderline Personality Disorder in Male and Female Offenders Newly Committed to Prison," *Comprehensive Psychiatry* 48, no. 5 (September–October 2007), 400–405.

13. This is the case of "Marge" documented by Gail Atlas, Catherine G. Fine, and Richard Kluft in "Multiple Personality Disorder Misdiagnosed as Mental Retardation: a Case Report," *Dissociation* 1, no. 1 (March 1988), 77–83.

Glossary

Adaptationalism: An approach to treatment for dissociative identity disorder in which the goal is not necessarily *integration* (see below), but rather helping patients manage their lives more smoothly and function more effectively.

Affect: An expressed emotion; for example, if anger is the emotion, then the demonstration of anger through body language and/or words could be stated, "He had an angry affect."

Affiliative learner: Someone who takes in the teachings of those with whom he feels a strong affiliation, without needing to expose those teachings to critical evaluation; this learning style is typical of Dionysian devotees in various disciplines—religion, science, politics, and so on (see also *Dionysian*).

Agoraphobia: Fear of not being able to cope with a strange or crowded environment from which it could be hard to escape; afflicted persons remain "safely" at home in order to avoid the "unacceptable" risk of venturing out into the world.

Alexithymia: A condition of having trouble identifying and or expressing in words the emotion one is experiencing.

Alter: An abbreviated way of saying "alter-personality" or "alternate personality;" a person with dissociative identity disorder experiences a fracturing of the core personality into alters that help the traumatized person adapt by assuming responsibility for certain emotions, memories, and behaviors that the person cannot handle.

Apollonian: As described by Herbert Spiegel, MD, and David Spiegel, MD, in *Trance and Treatment*, such an individual is characterized by reason over passion; someone associated with a low trance capacity, therefore, not given to dissociative experiences

Assimilative learner: Someone who critically evaluates every concept before being able to embrace it as truth, a typical Apollonian style (See also *Apollonian*).

Borderline personality: A condition in which the person manifests extremes of emotion and corresponding behavior, and likely has its roots in severe childhood trauma.

Catecholamine hypothesis: A theory of the biochemical causes of mental illnesses such as depression and schizophrenia, that involves neurochemicals in the catecholamine family, such as dopamine (see also *dopamine*).

Cluster A: A DSM-IV category of personality disorders that includes schizoid, schizotypal, and paranoid personalities.

Cluster B: A DSM-IV category of personality disorders that includes borderline personalities, narcissistic personalities, and antisocial personalities.

Cluster C: A DSM-IV category of personality disorders that includes avoidance, passive-aggressive, obsessive-compulsive, and other disorders associated with people who are higher functioning than those with disorders in Cluster A or B.

Comorbidity: A state of living with two or more illnesses at once.

Compromise formation: An attitude, belief, behavior, and so on that serves to take care of opposing needs simultaneously; compromise formation is a mostly automatic, unconscious process, and many mental symptoms can be partially understood as compromise formations, including the development of alters.

Confabulation: Using fictitious material to fill in unremembered gaps in a story, e.g., an alcoholic's attempt to make sense of an event when he can't remember what happened.

Conversion disorder: Characterized by "symptoms" that have no basis in disease or injury, but both the production of the symptoms and the motivation are unconscious to the patient.

Corrective emotional experience: Revising feelings to get them more in line with reality: for example, a patient's learning to feel that the therapist honestly does care and respects her, rather than feeling that he, like her parents as she experienced them, is just tolerating her presence.

Daydreaming: A type of dissociation experienced by many people who are mentally healthy.

Déjà vu: A kind of depersonalization/derealization experience in which a person is in a place or a situation that is new, yet there is an intense familiarity to it; the person may even have a sense of being able to predict what happens next.

Depersonalization disorder: A disorder in which the person gets a repeated or persistent feeling of being detached from his or her own mental processes or body; depersonalization experiences are rather common, but harmless unless they create distress or disability.

Derealization: A dissociative phenomenon in which a person perceives circumstances as in a dream or in a fog.

***Diagnostic and Statistical Manual of Mental Disorders* (DSM)**: A publication of the American Psychiatric Association, the DSM provides the common terms and standards for the classification of mental disorders; first published in 1952, it has been updated periodically since then.

Disinhibition: A lack of restraint that involves disregard for social conventions and generally involves a level of risk taking that seems devoid of judgment.

Dissociative amnesia: A condition in which a person lacks the ability to recall important personal information; usually associated with a repeated unpleasant experience in childhood rather than a single event (see also *psychogenic amnesia*).

Dissociative band theory: A theory about the nature of dissociation, from normal to disorder, conceived of by Saroj Parida, MD, and developed in conjunction with him by the authors.

Dissociative fugue: A departure to a different state of mind as well as a different physical location; in the fugue state, the person is disconnected from awareness of behavior or location (see also *psychogenic fugue*).

Dissociative identity disorder (DID): Formerly known as multiple personality disorder, it is a condition stemming from childhood trauma in which the person partially fractures mentally into different people in a way, but may well maintain the ability to perform intellectually demanding tasks on a daily basis.

Dopamine: A neurotransmitter chemical that affects a broad range of functions in the brain, including the experience of intense pleasure (see also *Catecholamine hypothesis*).

Dionysian: As described by Herbert Spiegel, MD, and David Spiegel, MD, in *Trance and Treatment*, such an individual is characterized by passion over reason; someone associated with a high trance capacity, and therefore, given to dissociative experiences.

Factitious disorder: Characterized by "symptoms" consciously generated by a person, but without conscious awareness and understanding of the motive.

Focal awareness: A kind of "tunnel vision" that is an essential part of a trance state.

Frontal disinhibition: Temporary or permanent impairment of exercise of social judgment mediated by the frontal lobes of the brain, usually due to drug or alcohol intoxication or brain disease or injury, respectively.

Frontal release behavior: Unrestrained behavior in which the frontal cortex of the brain that mediates conscience and executive functions, such as knowing how to behave, is impaired or disconnected from other brain regions, such as the emotional brain (see also *disinhibition*).

Frontotemporal dementia: A type of dementia in which disinhibition is often a particularly salient feature (see also *frontal disinhibition*).

Global assessment of functioning (GAF): A numerical score, from 1 to 99, which indicates how well a person is doing in the world; it is Axis V of a five-part psychiatric diagnosis.

Highway hypnosis: A lay expression for the common experience of trance (hypnotic) states while driving a car, such that certain important sensory cues, such as exit signs, are dissociated from conscious perception and "missed."

Hyperthymic temperament: An inborn temperament characterized by unusually great physical and mental energy and elevated mood.

Hypnagogic hallucinations: Relatively common depersonalization/derealization experiences that occur as a person is drifting off to sleep, experienced as "dreaming while awake."

Hypnopompic hallucinations: Depersonalization/derealization experiences that occur as a person is waking up; the waking up equivalent of hypnagogic hallucinations.

Hypnosis: An intentional trance state.

Hippocampus: A deep brain structure, usually considered part of the "emotional brain," responsible for the recording and storage of memory.

Integration: The healing state for a person with dissociative identity disorder in which the personalities return to a relatively unified state; also refers to stages of personality development in early childhood.

Isakower phenomenon: An experience in which a person's sense of personal boundary expands and/or contracts in an unsettling manner; named after the psychoanalyst Otto Isakower who described it in a 1936 article on mental disorders associated with falling asleep.

Jamais vu: A kind of depersonalization/derealization experience in which a person is in a place or situation where he/she has been many times before, but with a complete lack of familiarity.

Malignant narcissism: A personality disorder characterized by self-centeredness, self-absorption, and a belief that "I can do no wrong."

Malingering disorder: Characterized by "symptoms" manufactured by the patient, whose motive for symptom production is conscious to the person; a smart criminal who invents periods of amnesia in an attempt to "beat a rap" is malingering.

Meditation: An intentional act that may involve a self-hypnotic state of consciousness.

Odyssean: As described by Herbert Spiegel, MD, and David Spiegel, MD, in *Trance and Treatment*, such an individual falls between the Apollonian and Dionysian in terms of the interplay of reason and passion and in terms of trance capacity.

PACE: An acronym for playfulness, acceptance, curiosity, and empathy that summarizes the key elements of the therapeutic approach taken at the Quittie Glen Center for Mental Health; first coined by Daniel A. Hughes, MD.

Paranoid personality: One with an unremitting suspiciousness of all others.

Peripheral awareness: The opposite of "tunnel vision," it is a general awareness of surroundings that exists side-by-side with focal awareness, but is radically diminished during a trance state.

Peritraumatic dissociation: Dissociation that occurs at or shortly after the traumatic event, thought by some experts to be a risk factor for later development of PTSD.

Personality disorder: In terms of the *Diagnostic and Statistical Manual of Mental Disorders*, a disorder falling into one of three categories of severity; comprising Axis II of a five-part psychiatric diagnosis.

Personification: The act of maintaining a memory of a traumatic event as part of one's "personal" history, rather than sticking the memory of the event somewhere deep and inaccessible within the unconscious mind, that is, dissociating it.

Premorbid personality: A state before the onset of mental illness.

Provisional diagnosis: A temporary, "working" diagnosis.

***Psychodynamic Diagnostic Manual* (PDM)**: Developed by psychoanalytic therapists wanting to contribute to a much more broad-based and meaningful diagnostic formulation for patients than the *Diagnostic and Statistical Manual of Mental Disorders* alone provides; first published by the Alliance of Psychodynamic Organizations in 2006.

Psychodynamic psychotherapy: A "talk therapy" approach based on psychoanalytic principles, aimed at healing by discovery of the influence of past experiences and relationships on current mental life and relationships.

Psychogenic amnesia: A condition in which a person lacks the ability to recall important personal information; usually associated with a repeated unpleasant experience in childhood rather than a single event (see also *dissociative amnesia*).

Psychogenic fugue: A departure to a different state of mind as well as a different physical location; in the fugue state, the person is disconnected from awareness of behavior or location (See also *dissociative fugue*).

Psychosocial stressors: Any current or historical environmental circumstances that bear upon the person's mental illness, such as death of a loved one, academic failure, and so on.

R/O: Medical shorthand for "rule out," a note that reminds the clinician to assess further for the possibility of a particular disorder; e.g., R/O panic disorder (for a person presenting with acute anxiety).

Relational psychoanalysis: A type of psychoanalysis that emphasizes the role of both real and imagined relationships in mental illness and healing, and therefore at times will bring the feelings of the therapist actively into the therapy for mutual reflection by patient and therapist.

Reparenting: An approach to DID therapy that treats the alters like individual people.

Schizoid personality: A severe and potentially disabling personality disorder whose sufferers can at times experience significant breaks with reality.

Schizotypal personality: A severe and potentially disabling personality disorder marked by extreme social awkwardness and the presence of unusual beliefs and behavioral oddities.

State-dependent memory: Memory of events or circumstances that occurred during an altered state of mind, that may be retrieved by returning to that state of mind; for example, a memory formed in a drunken state might only be retrievable in a drunken state.

Structural Cluster Survey: An assessment to help determine how readily a person can experience the therapeutic benefits of hypnosis.

Talk therapy: A casual label for psychotherapies that involve conversation and interaction between therapist and patient.

Temperament: Inborn predispositions toward feeling and behaving in certain ways, estimated to affect up to 50 percent of personality development.

Visualization: A type of normal dissociation in which the "mind's eye" of a person sees that person doing a particular task or sequence of actions; it is often used by athletes to rehearse mentally.

Bibliography

Allen, John J. B., and Hallam L. Movius. "The Objective Assessment of Amnesia in Dissociative Identity Disorder Using Event-related Potentials." *International Journal of Psychophysiology* 38, no. 1 (2000): 21–41. http://dx.doi.org/10.1016/S0167-8760(00)00128-8.

Alliance of Psychodynamic Organizations. *Psychodynamic Diagnostic Manual (PDM)*. 1st ed. Bethesda, MD: Alliance of Psychodynamic Organizations, 2006. American Psychiatric Association. *Diagnostic and Statistical Manual of Mental Disorders, Fourth Edition (Text Revision)*. Washington, DC: American Psychiatric Publishing, 2000.

Chess, Stella, and Alexander Thomas. *Temperament: Theory and Practice*. New York: Routledge, 1996.

Christoff, Kalina, Alan M. Gordon, Jonathan Smallwood, Rachelle Smith, and Jonathan W. Schooler. "Experience Sampling during fMRI Reveals Default Network and Executive System Contributions to Mind Wandering." *Proceedings of the National Academy of Sciences of the United States* 106, no. 21 (May 2009): 8719–24. doi:10.1073/pnas.0900234106.

Damásio, A. R., B. J. Everitt, and D. Bishop. "The Somatic Marker Hypothesis and the Possible Functions of the Prefrontal Cortex [and Discussion]." *Philosophical Transactions of the Royal Society of London Series B: Biological Sciences* 351, no. 1346 (October 1996): 1413–20. doi:10.1098/rstb.1996.0125.

Eich, James Eric. "The Cue-dependent Nature of State-dependent Retrieval." *Memory and Cognition* 8, no. 2 (1980): 157–73. Frewen, Paul A., and Ruth A. Lanius. "Neurobiology of Dissociation: Unity and Disunity in Mind-Body-Brain." *Psychiatric Clinics of North America* 29 (2006): 113–28.

Hartley, Gregory, and Maryann Karinch. *Get People to Do What You Want*. Franklin Lakes, NJ: Career Press, 2008. Hughes, Daniel A. *Attachment-Focused Family Therapy Workbook*. New York: W.W. Norton, 2011.

Kluft, Richard P. "Basic Principles in Conducting the Psychotherapy of Multiple Personality Disorder." In Richard P. Kluft and Catherine G. Fine (eds.), *Clinical*

Perspectives on Multiple Personality Disorder, 19–50. Washington, DC: American Psychiatric Publishing, 1993.

Lagopoulos, Jim, Jian Xu, Inge Rasmussen, Alexandra Vik, Gin S. Malhi, Carl F. Eliassen, Ingrid E. Arntsen, Jardar G. Sæther, Stig Hollup, Are Holen, Svend Davanger, and Øyvind Ellingsen. "Increased Theta and Alpha EEG Activity during Nondirective Meditation." *The Journal of Alternative and Complementary Medicine* 15, no. 11 (November 2009): 1187–92. doi:10.1089/acm.2009.0113.

Leong, Stephanie, Wendi Waits, and Carroll Diebold. "Dissociative Amnesia and DSM-IV-TR Cluster C Personality Traits." *Psychiatry* 3, no. 1 (January 2006), 51–55.

Madow, Leo. *Love: How to Understand and Enjoy It*. New York: MacMillan, 1983.

Newberg, A. B., and E. G. d'Aquili. "The Neuropsychology of Religious and Spiritual Experience." *Journal of Consciousness Studies* 7, nos.11–12 (November–December 2000): 251–66.

Nijenhuis, Ellert, Onno van der Hart, and Kathy Steele. "Trauma-Related Structural Dissociation of the Personality." *Activitas Nervosa Superior* 52, no.1 (2010): 1–23. http://www.activitas.org/index.php/nervosa/article/view/81/125.

Oxnam, Robert B. *A Fractured Mind: My Life with Multiple Personality Disorder*. New York: Hyperion, 2005.

Spiegel, Herbert, and David Spiegel. *Trance and Treatment*. 2nd ed. Washington, DC: American Psychiatric Publishing, 2004.

Stark, Martha. *Modes of Therapeutic Action*. Northvale, NJ: Jason Aronson, 1999.

Stout, Martha. *The Myth of Sanity*. New York: Viking Penguin, 2001.

van der Kolk, Bessel A., Alexander C. McFarlane, and Lars Weisaeth, eds. *Traumatic Stress: The Effects of Overwhelming Experience on Mind, Body, and Society*. New York: Guilford, 1996.

Vermetten, Eric, Christian Schmahl, Sanneke Lindner, Richard J. Loewenstein, and J. Douglas Bremner. "Hippocampal and Amygdalar Volumes in Dissociative Identity Disorder." *The American Journal of Psychiatry* 163, no. 4 (April 2006): 630–36.

West, Cameron. *First Person Plural*. New York: Hyperion, 1999.

Index

157

About the Authors

John A. Biever, MD, is a general and child/adolescent psychiatrist in private practice at the Quittie Glen Center for Mental Health in Annville, Pennsylvania. He is a founding faculty member of the Central Pennsylvania Institute for Mental Health, where he and other faculty members present educational and training programs intended to promote sound mental health throughout the mid-state region and beyond. He is a consultant in child psychiatry to the Pennsylvania State Office of Mental Health and Substance Abuse Services and a clinical associate professor of psychiatry at the Penn State University College of Medicine.

Maryann Karinch is the author or coauthor of eighteen books, most of which focus on human behavior. She has led specialized training in body language with the Department of Homeland Security, staff and faculty at George Mason University, and members and guests of the International Spy Museum. In 2004, Karinch founded The Rudy Agency, a literary agency specializing in nonfiction.